SONGS OF BLACK AND WHITE

Strange ink patterns in a nostalgic field

A coloring ART book for adults

by **Julian Trocaru**

First edition

October 2015

EDITOR'S FOREWORD

"SONGS OF BLACK AND WHITE- Strange ink patterns in a nostalgic field" is the first coloring book for adults design by Julian Trocaru.

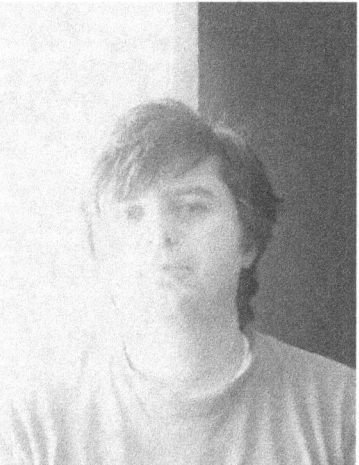

The approach used in drawing this book was one of an artist, every piece was thought and draw like a piece of **Art** in itself, a draw that nobody will be ashamed to put it on his house walls, and, even more, when you will put your own color on them, you will be even more proud showing it. The works done for this project could be consider unique because you cannot find something alike in coloring books for adults market and were done entirely by hand, not using a computer (the mirror effect or multiplication of patterns, like the majority of existing books) by avoiding the used patterns.

The inner idea (knowing how much work will require such a project) was that even if nobody will buy the drawings to color them, at least the artist will be proud to show them like a real part of his art work, so a win-win situation. The subjects of drawings are not unknown shapes, objects or animals, but they are treated in a different manner, a personal and unique manner.

In the author words:

"Till this April I never heard about coloring books for adults. The day I seen this domain exists and what impact had on people all around the world I said to myself: *This is something you can do too!*

The interaction of my art with people, an interaction at the level of creation (me the draw and them the color) not just them looking at my art is one thing I wanted for long time. So, I started in the same day trying to keep a balance between the small details and the overall design. Starting this project I had an eye on the two of authors, Peter Deligdisch and Johanna Basford. Both of them, for me, are the ones exceptional in this field.

The idea behind most of the works from this project is symmetry and multivalency. Symmetry for the peace that brings and multivalency for the beauty of multiple meanings that something could have.

I should add that for many years, since I am on the road of discovering my way in paintings, I always had, deep in me, a nostalgia of simplicity, a black and white nostalgia since my childhood...those times when I put the black pencil on white paper and instantly I was lost in fantastical realms of shapes, shapes that were born in my mostly unconscious mind. Discovering my way in paintings, the black and white adventure was left aside for many years...maybe too many years. So, when I seen the existence of *coloring books for adults*, I was, in a way, officially relieve...yes, I can express myself, again, just in black and white and people will enjoy working, coloring, on my works...what a beautiful gift an artist could receive!"

If you want to discover more works, art drawings and paintings of Julian Trocaru, you can find them here: www.juliantrocaru.com and more about this book project on his Julian Trocaru Facebook page.

Note: in the middle of the last drawing of this book you can add yourself whatever you will like...your portrait, somebody else portrait or anything else

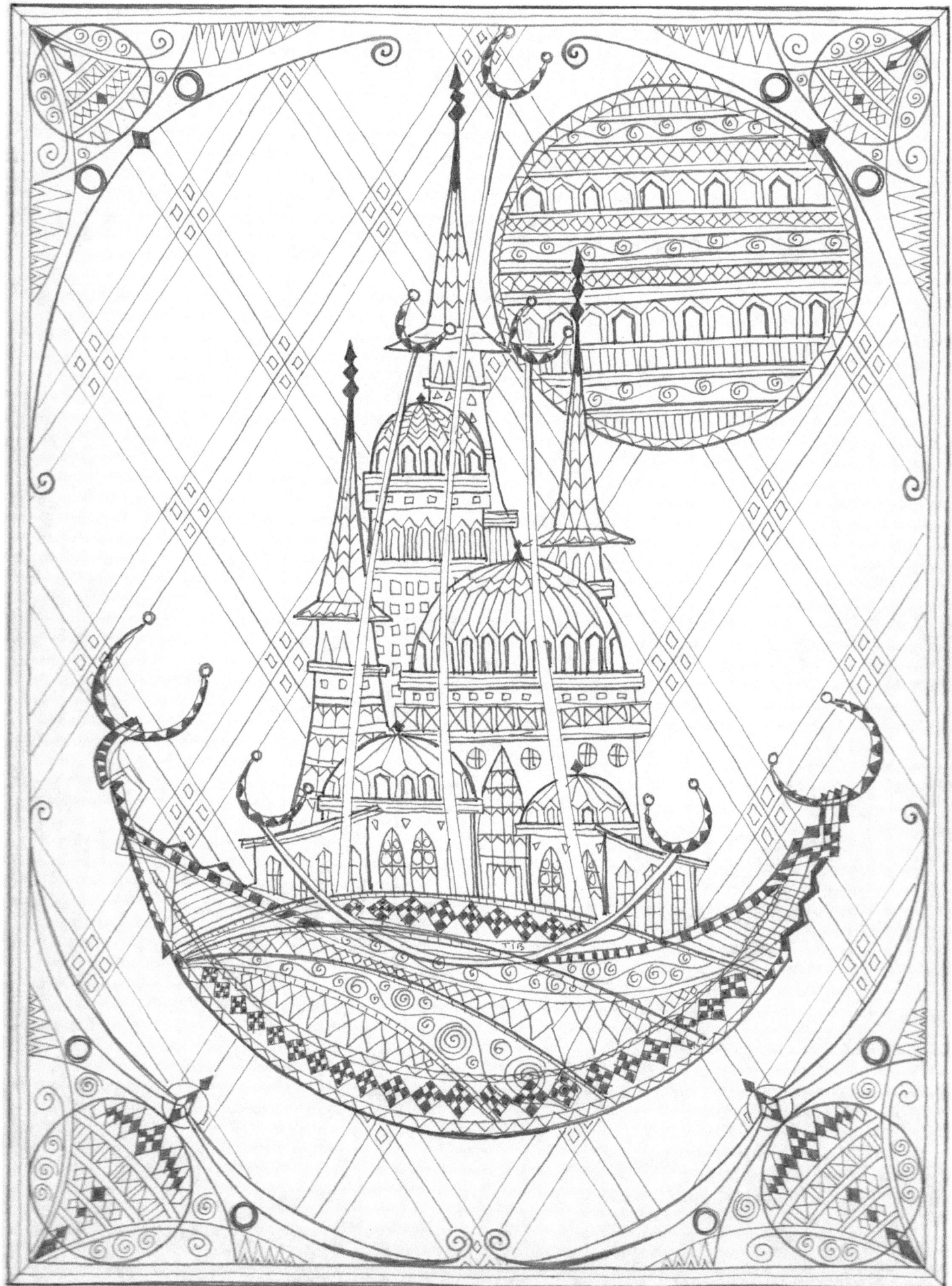

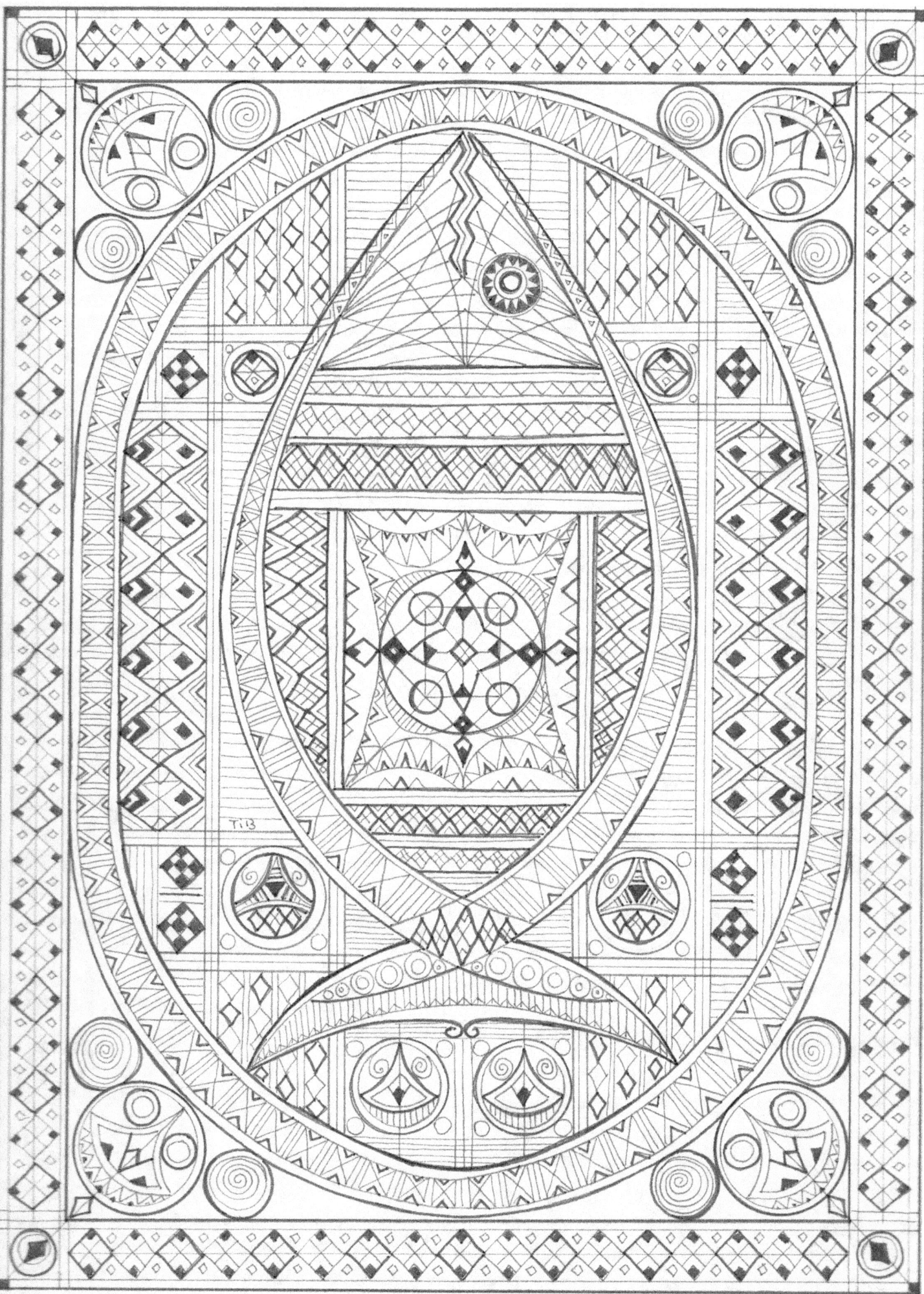

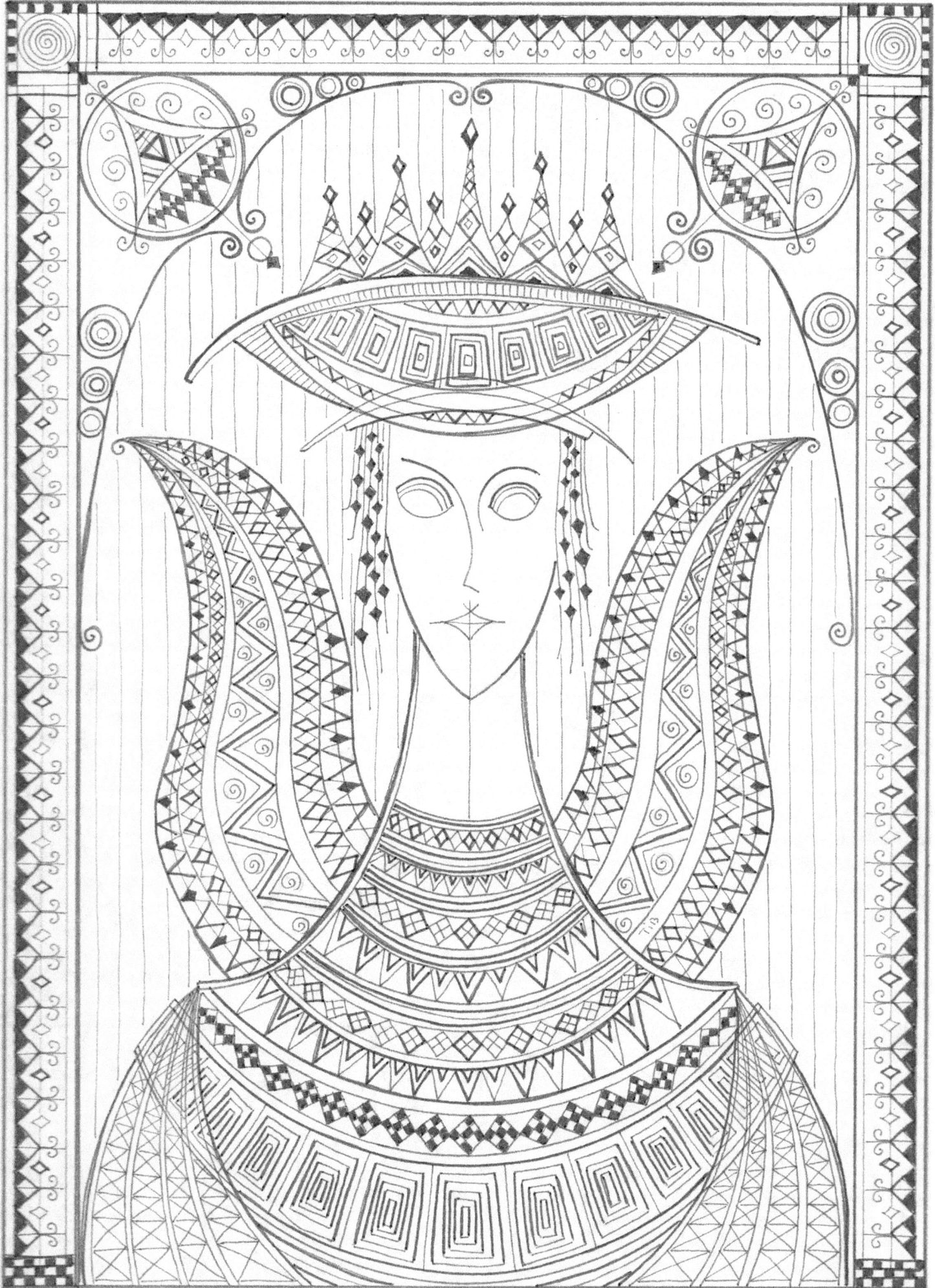

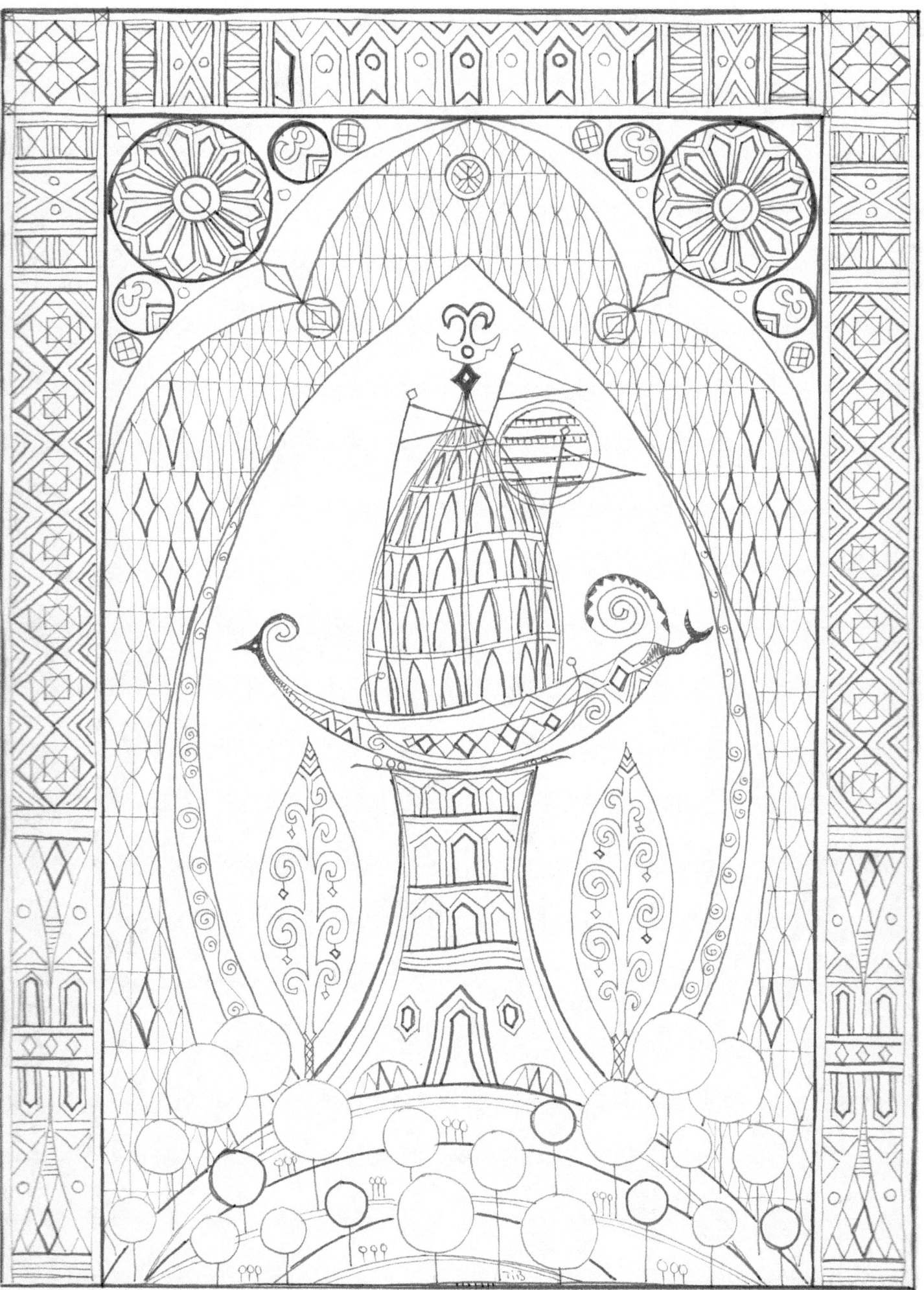

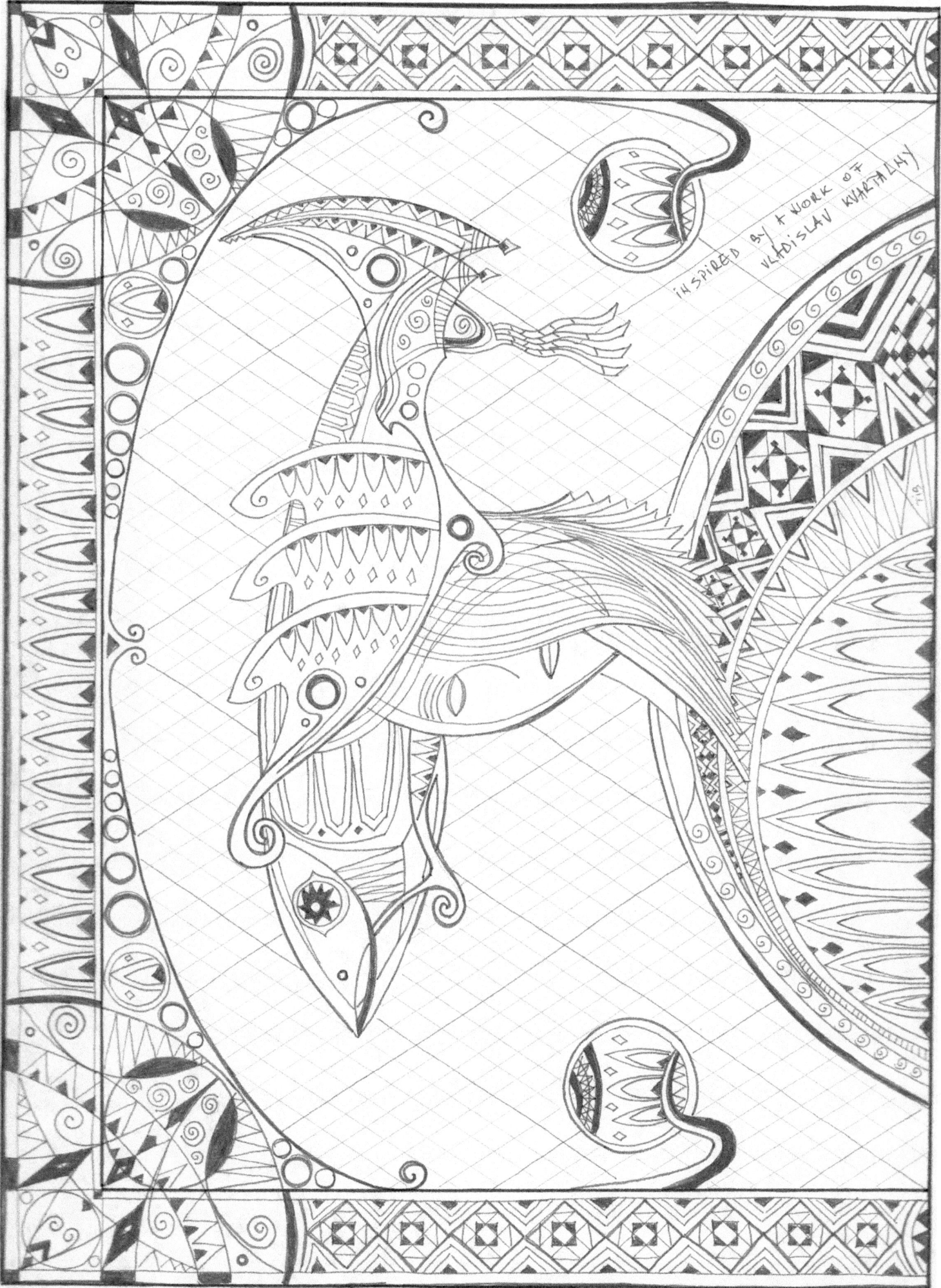

INSPIRED BY A WORK OF VLADISLAV KVARTALNY

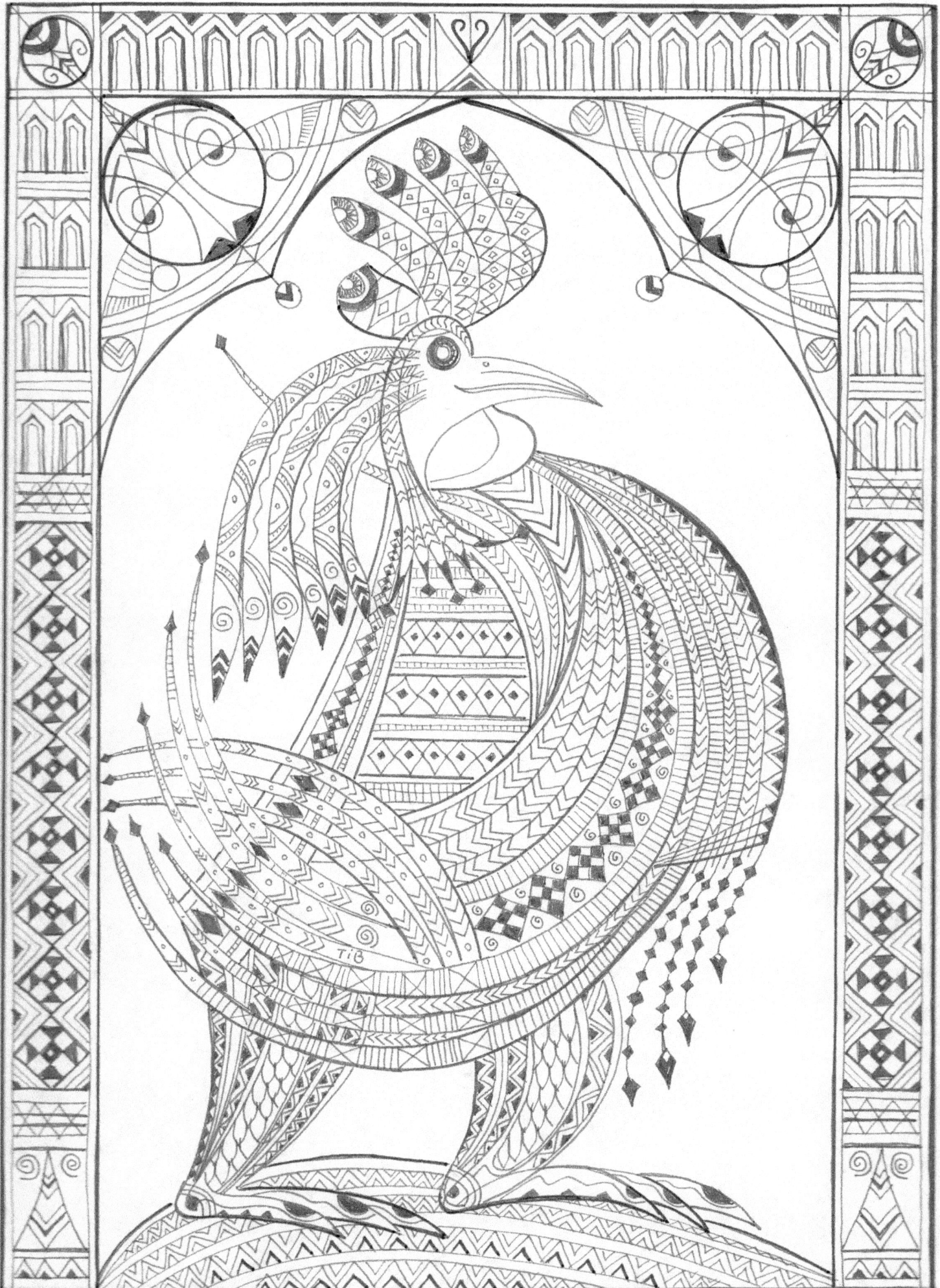

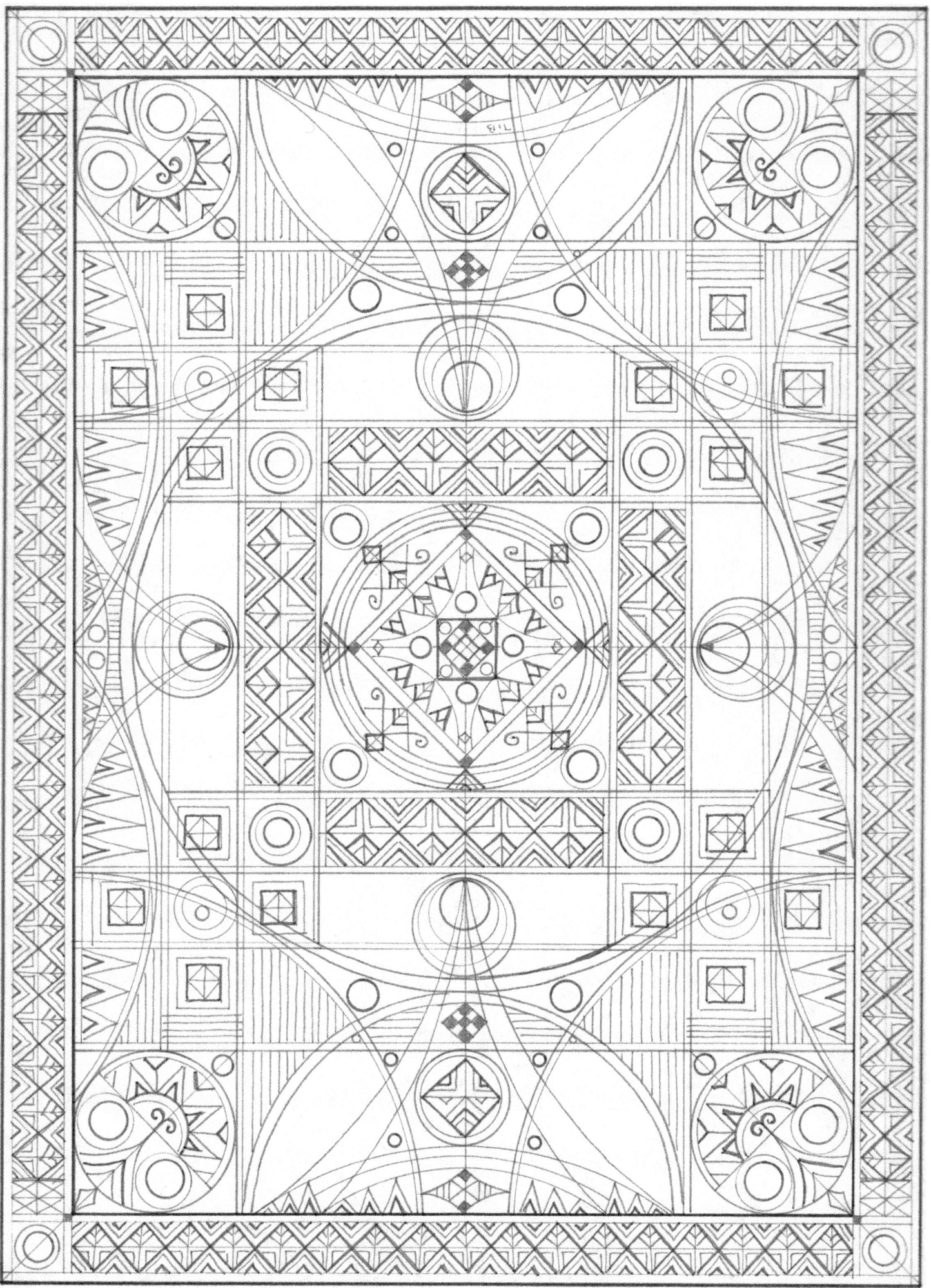

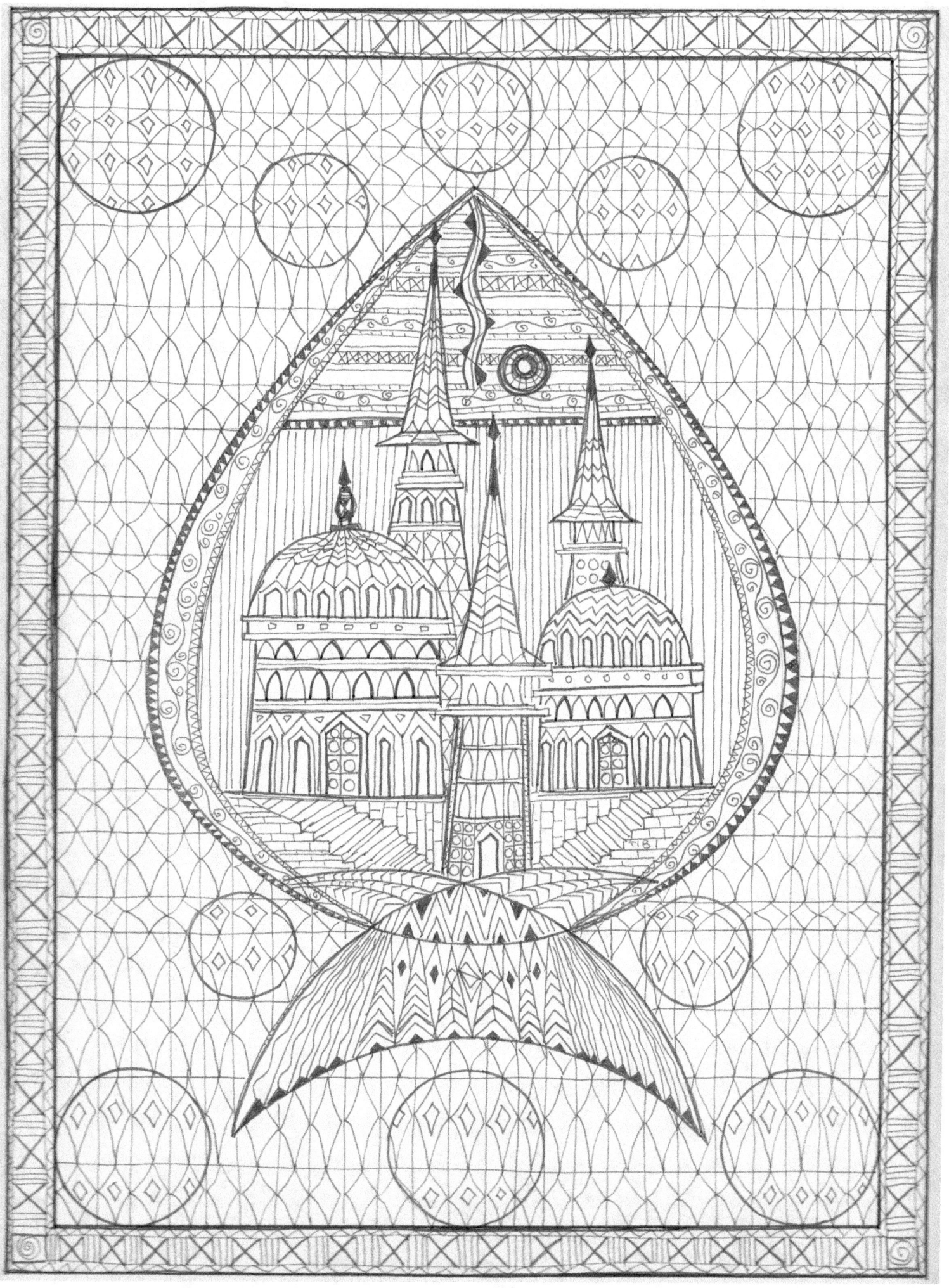

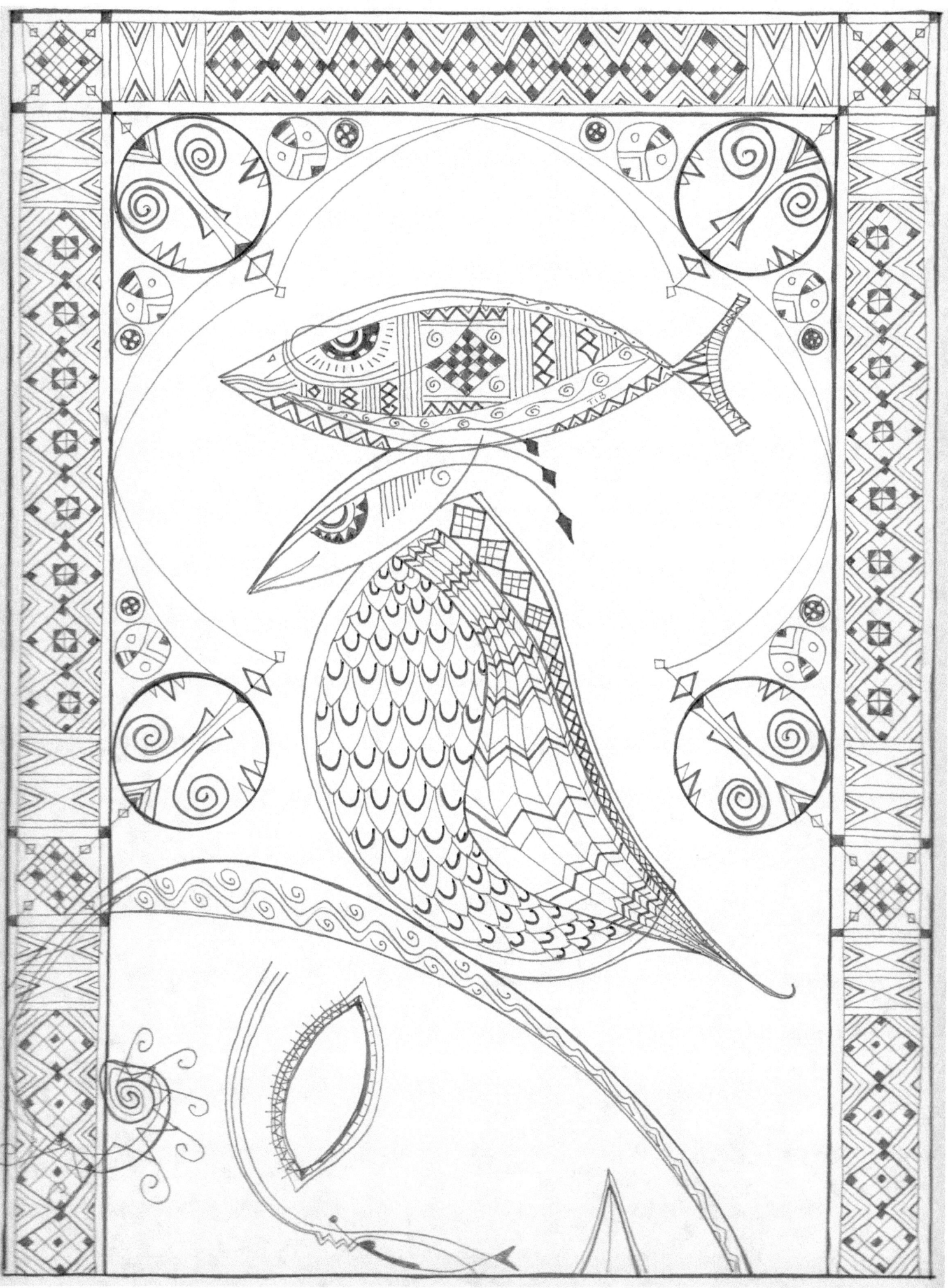

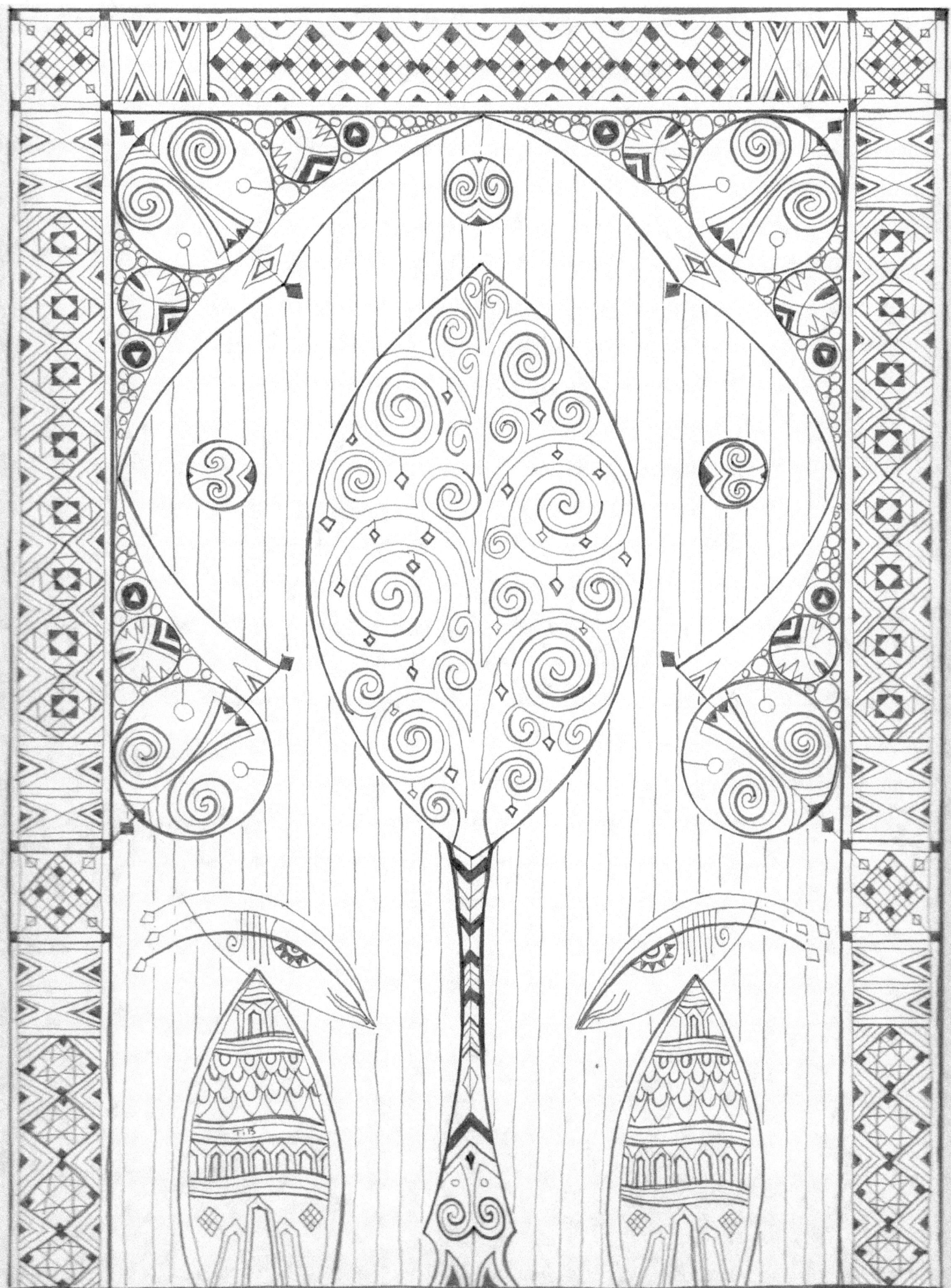

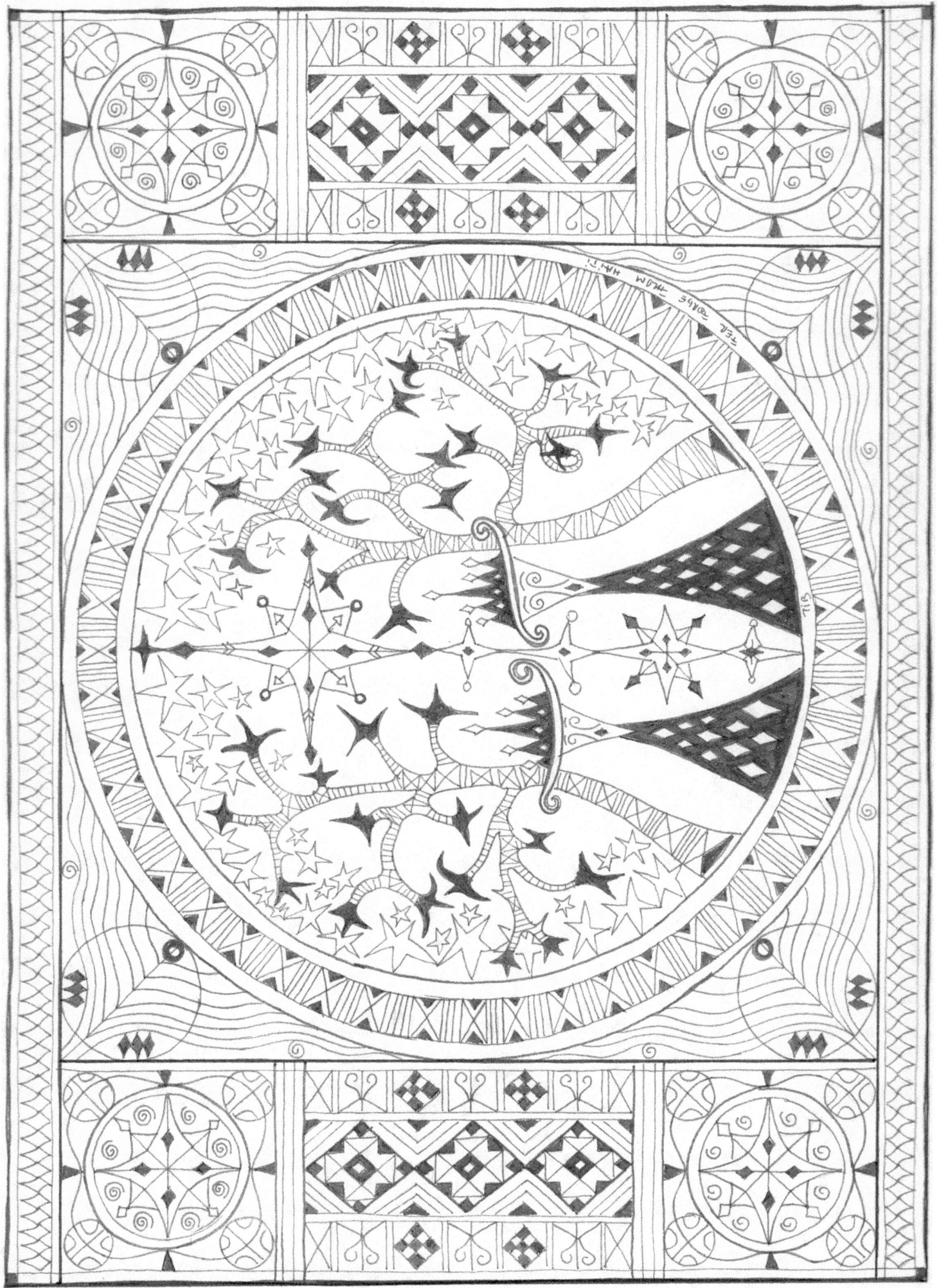

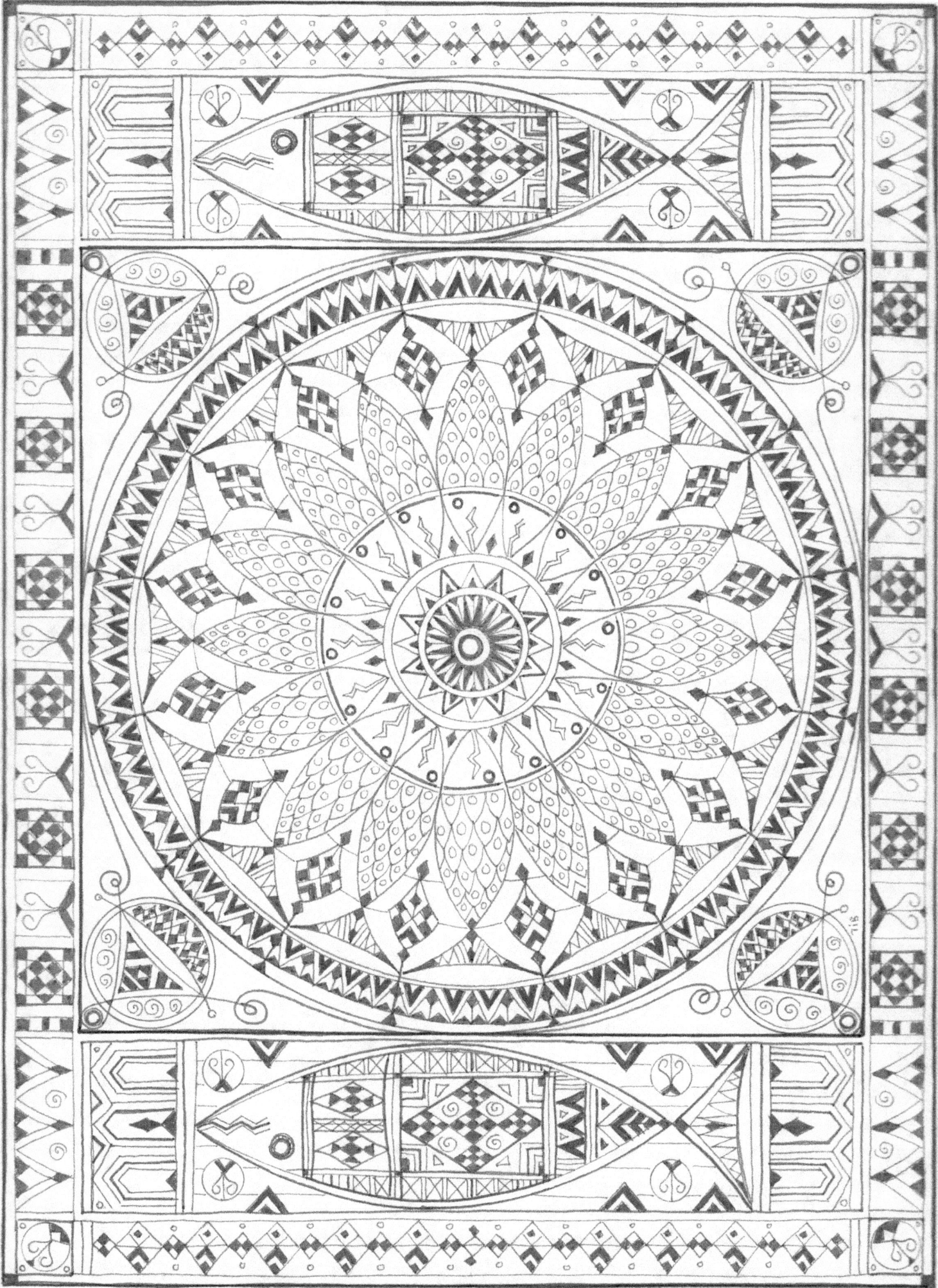

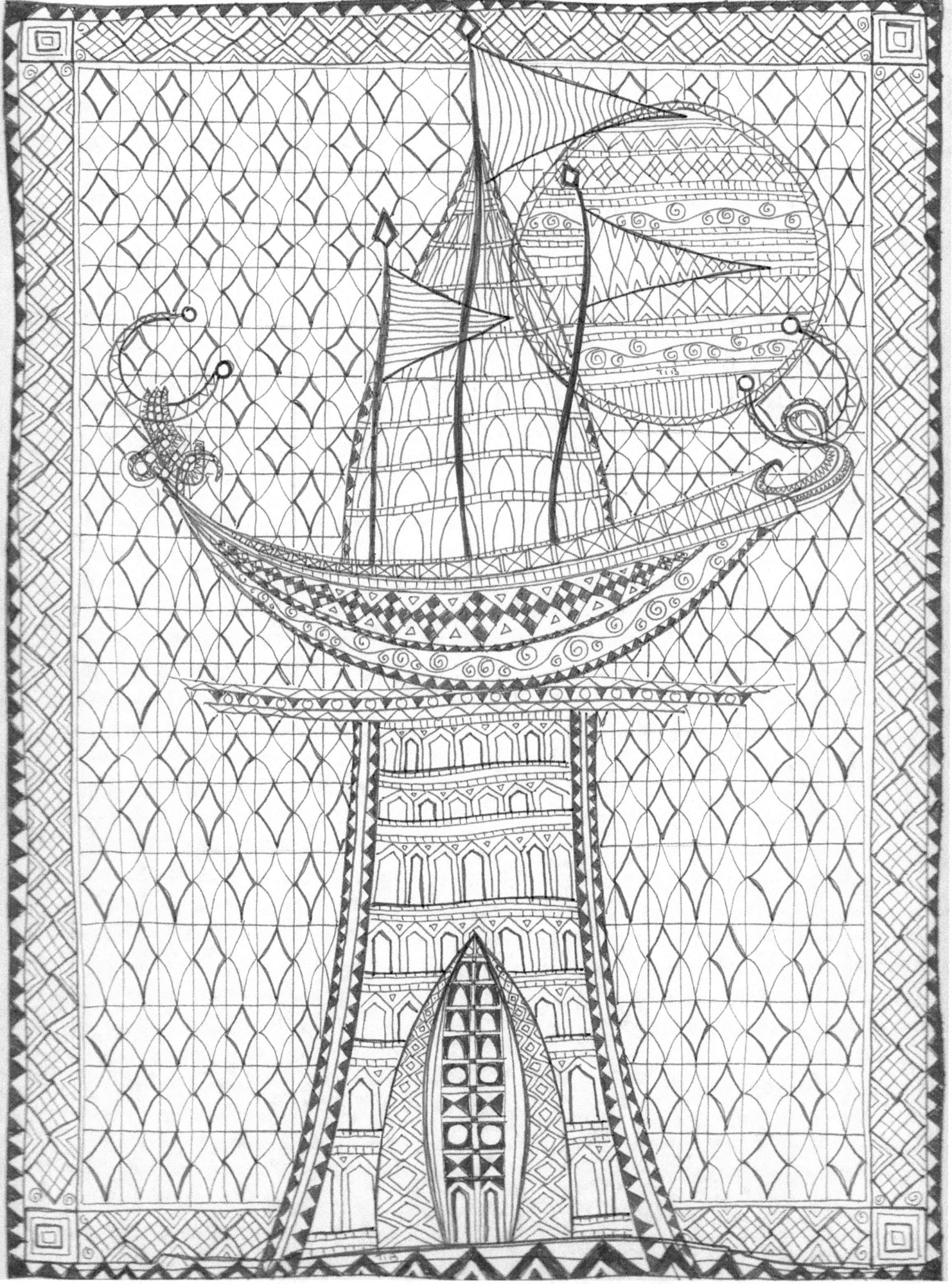

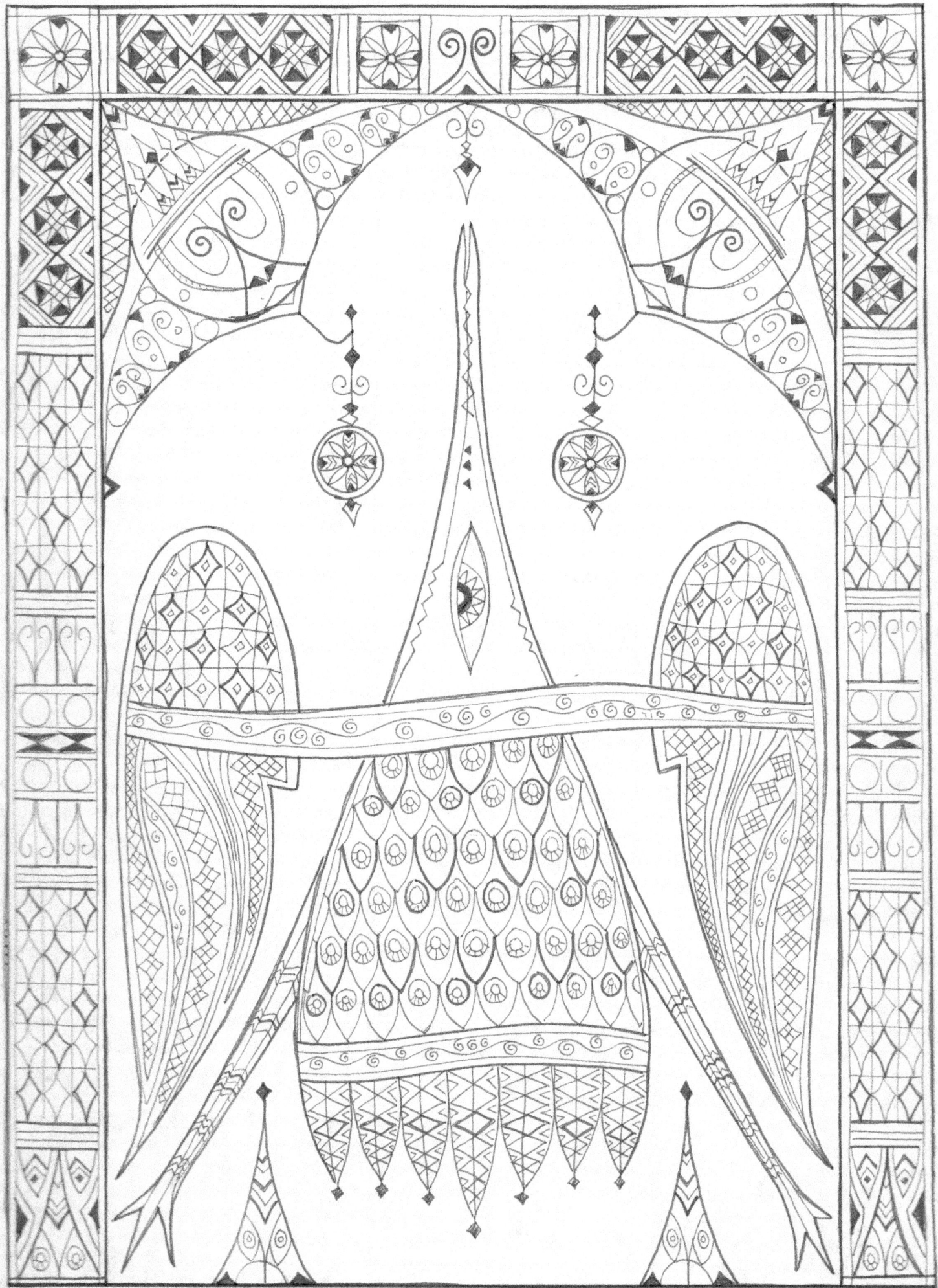

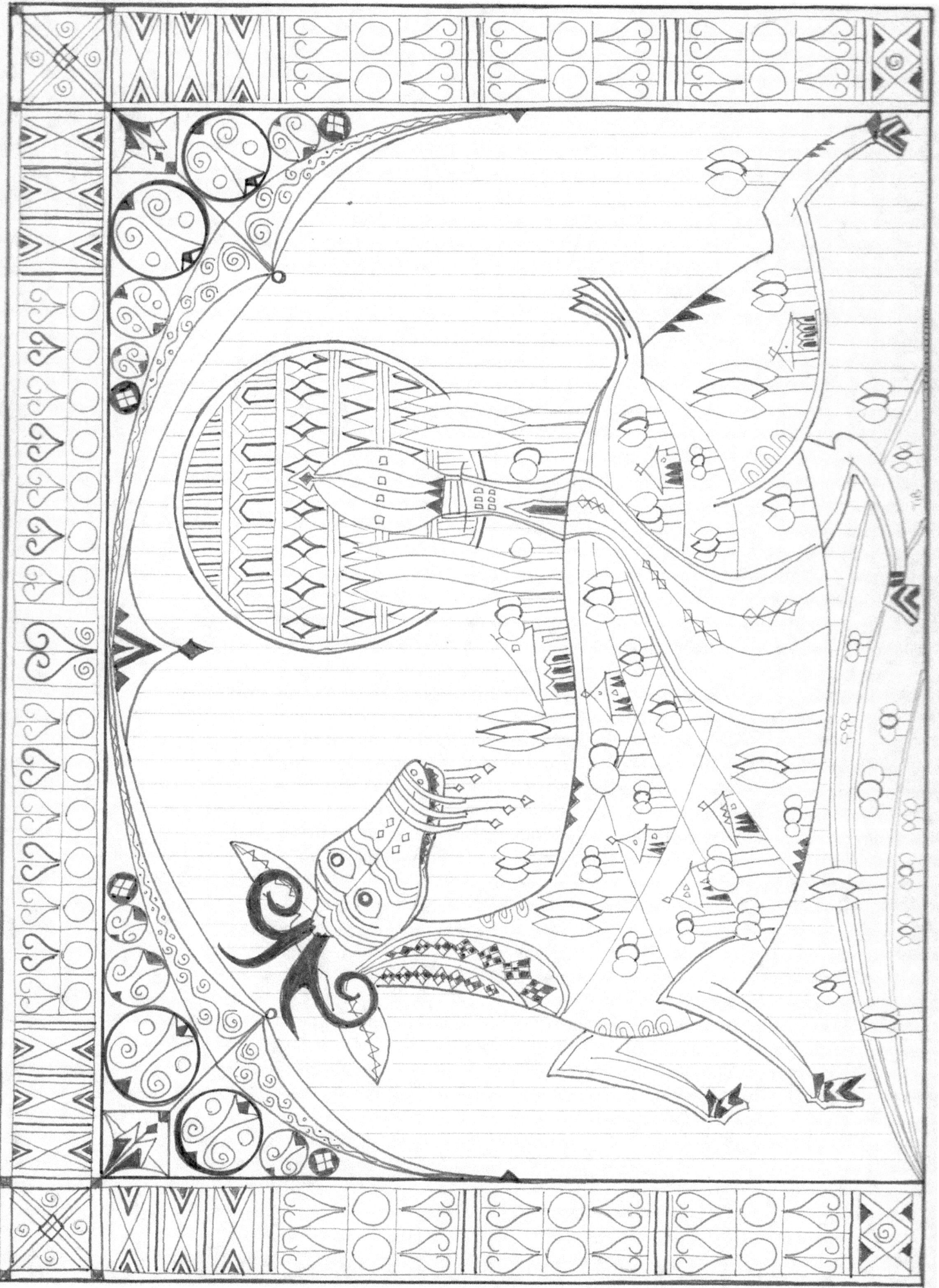

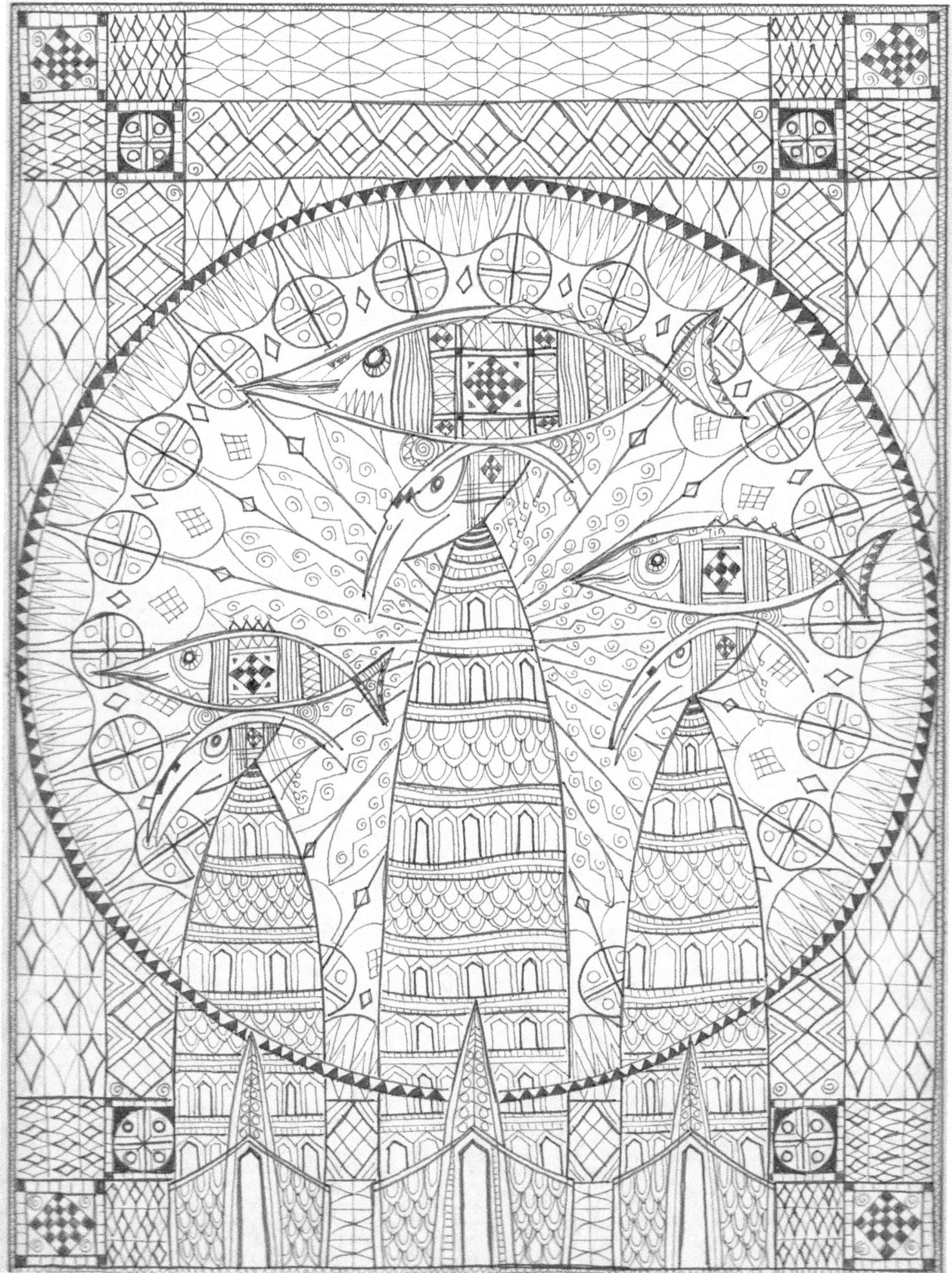

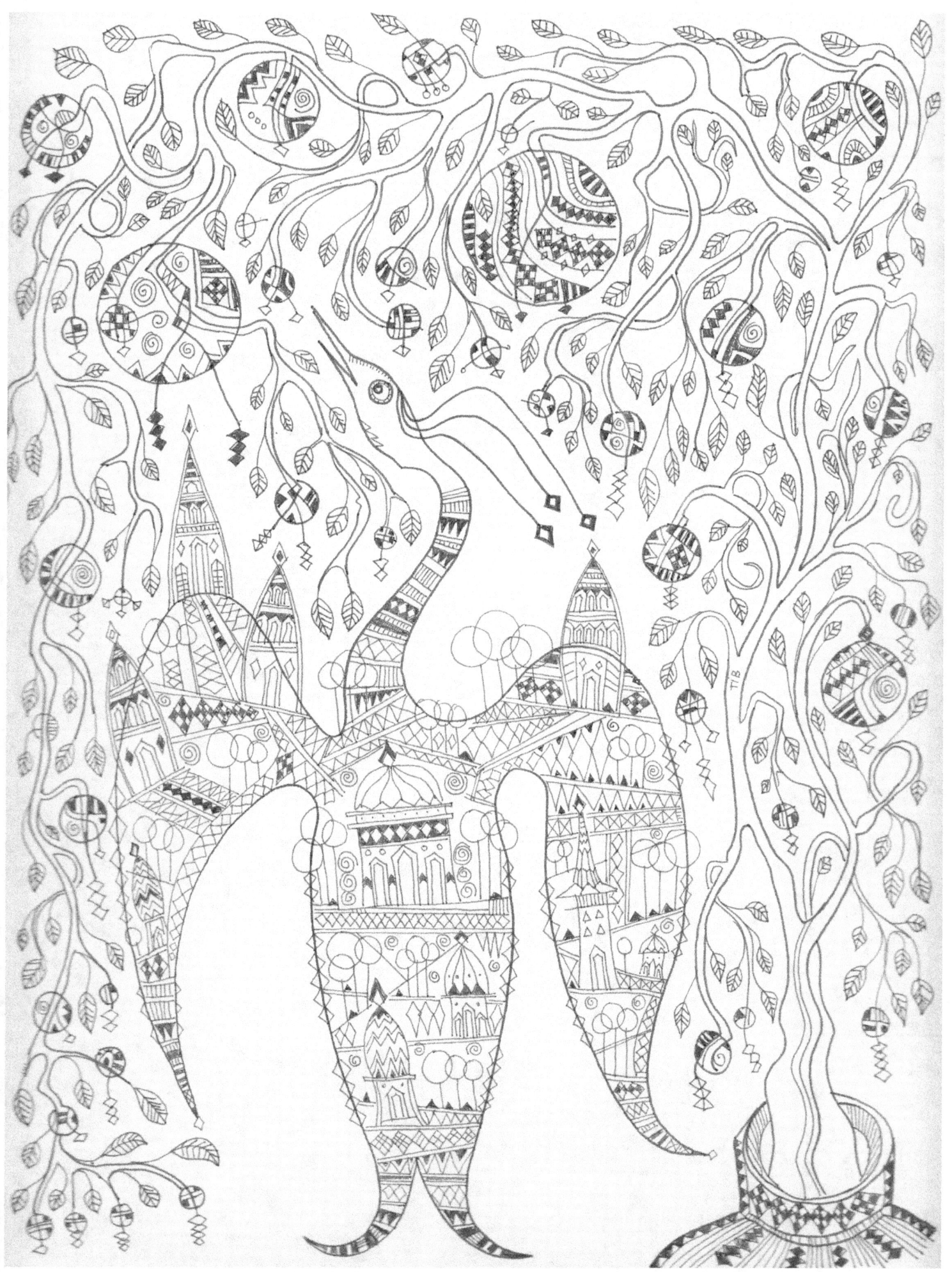

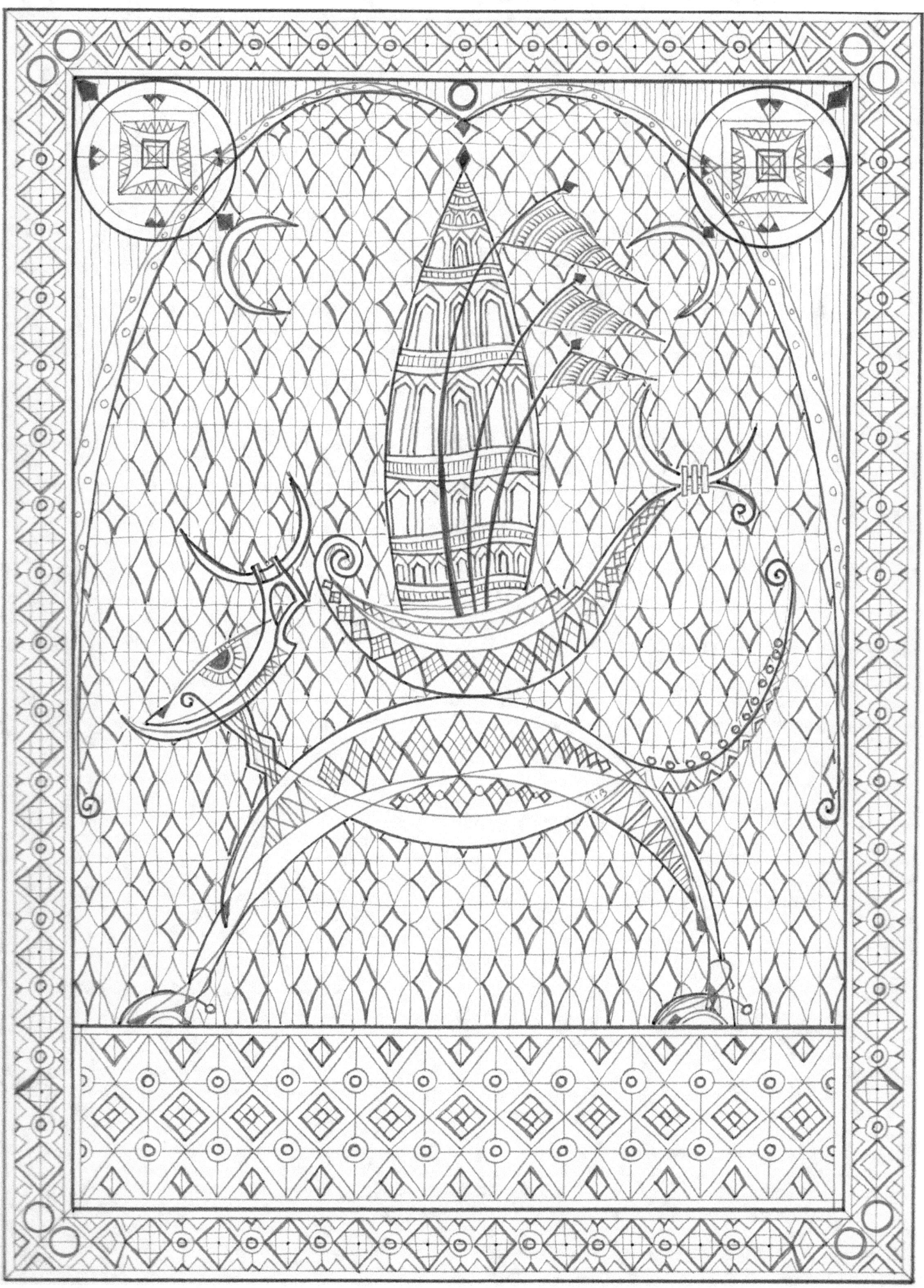

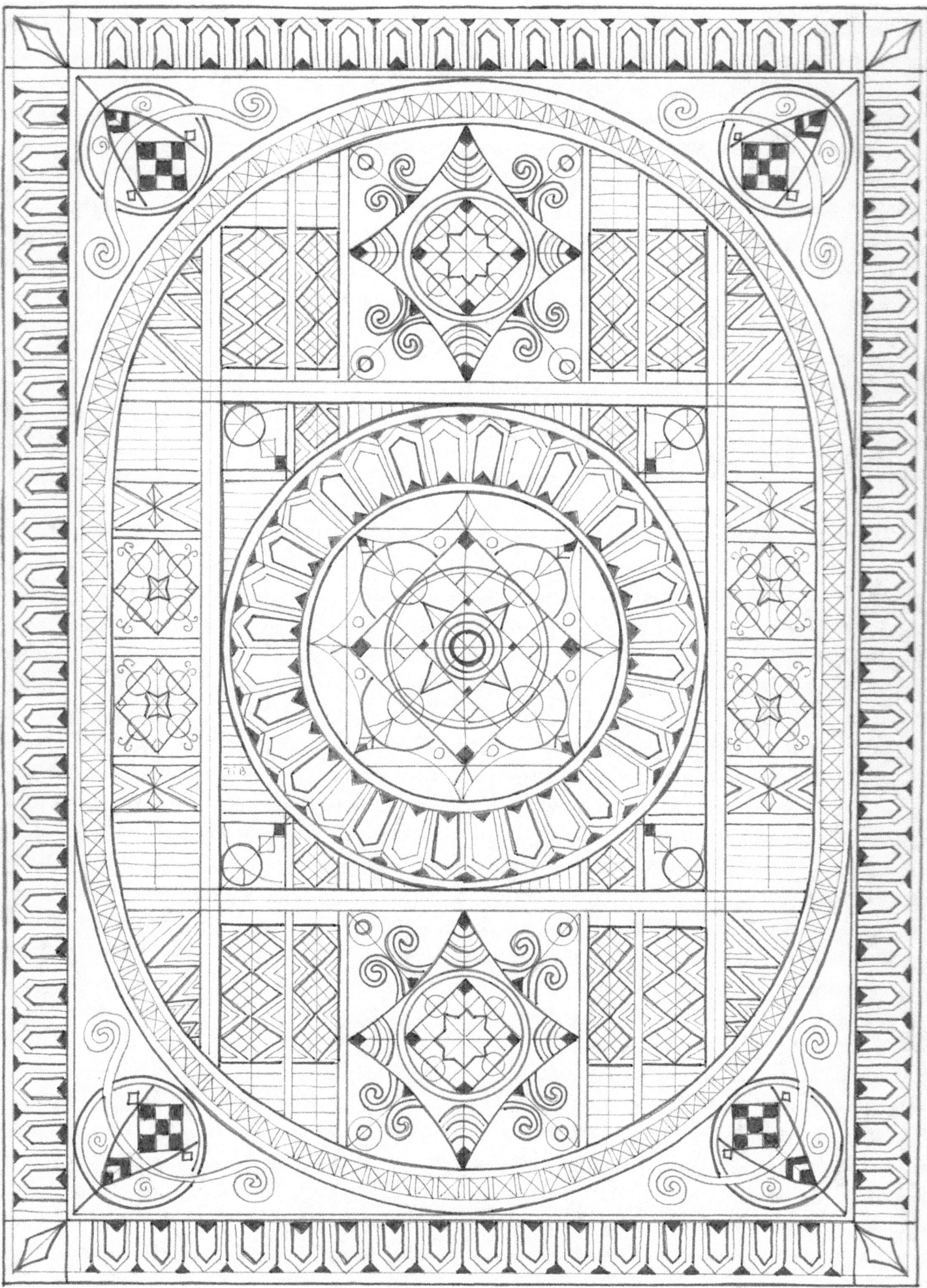

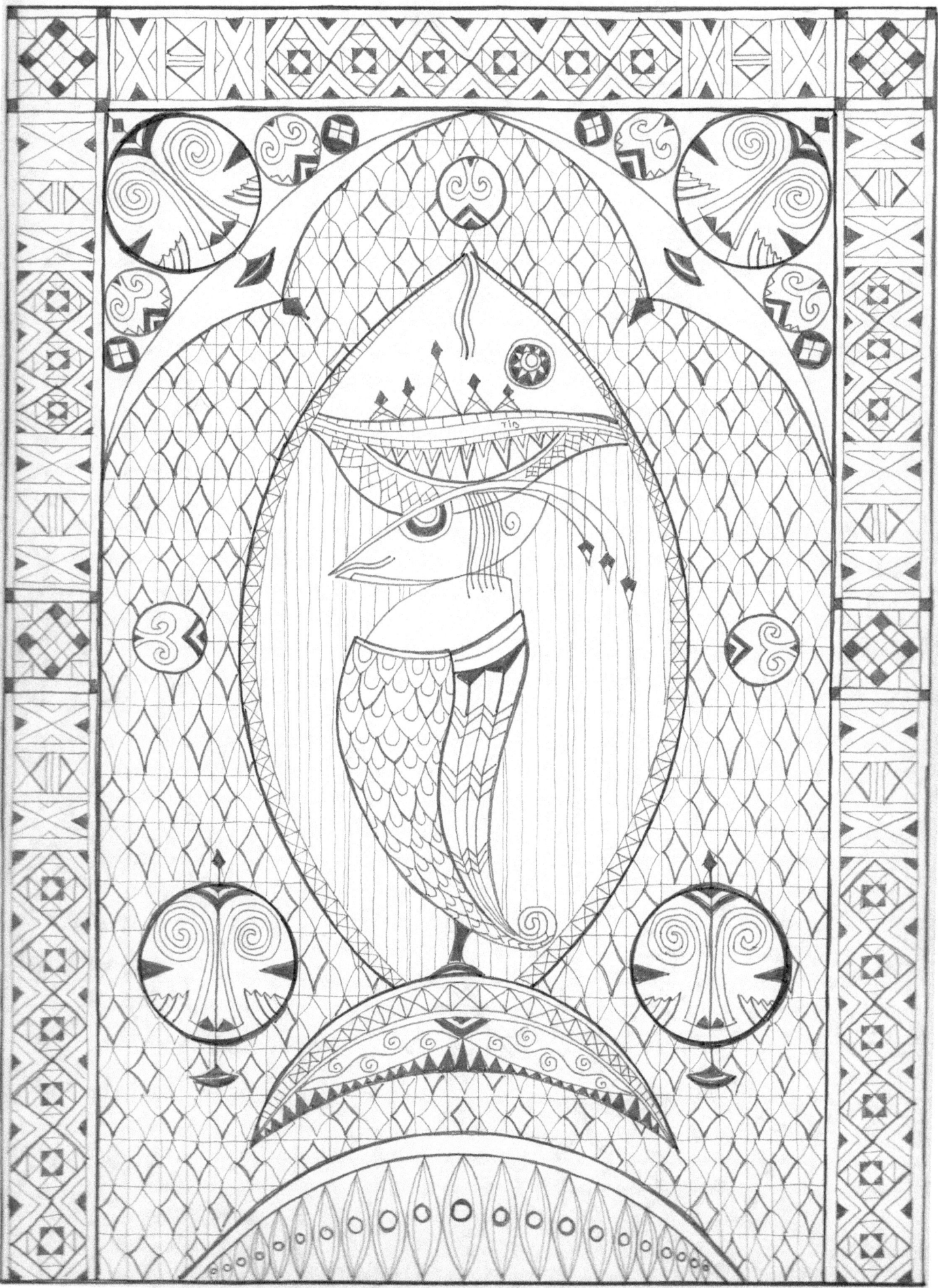

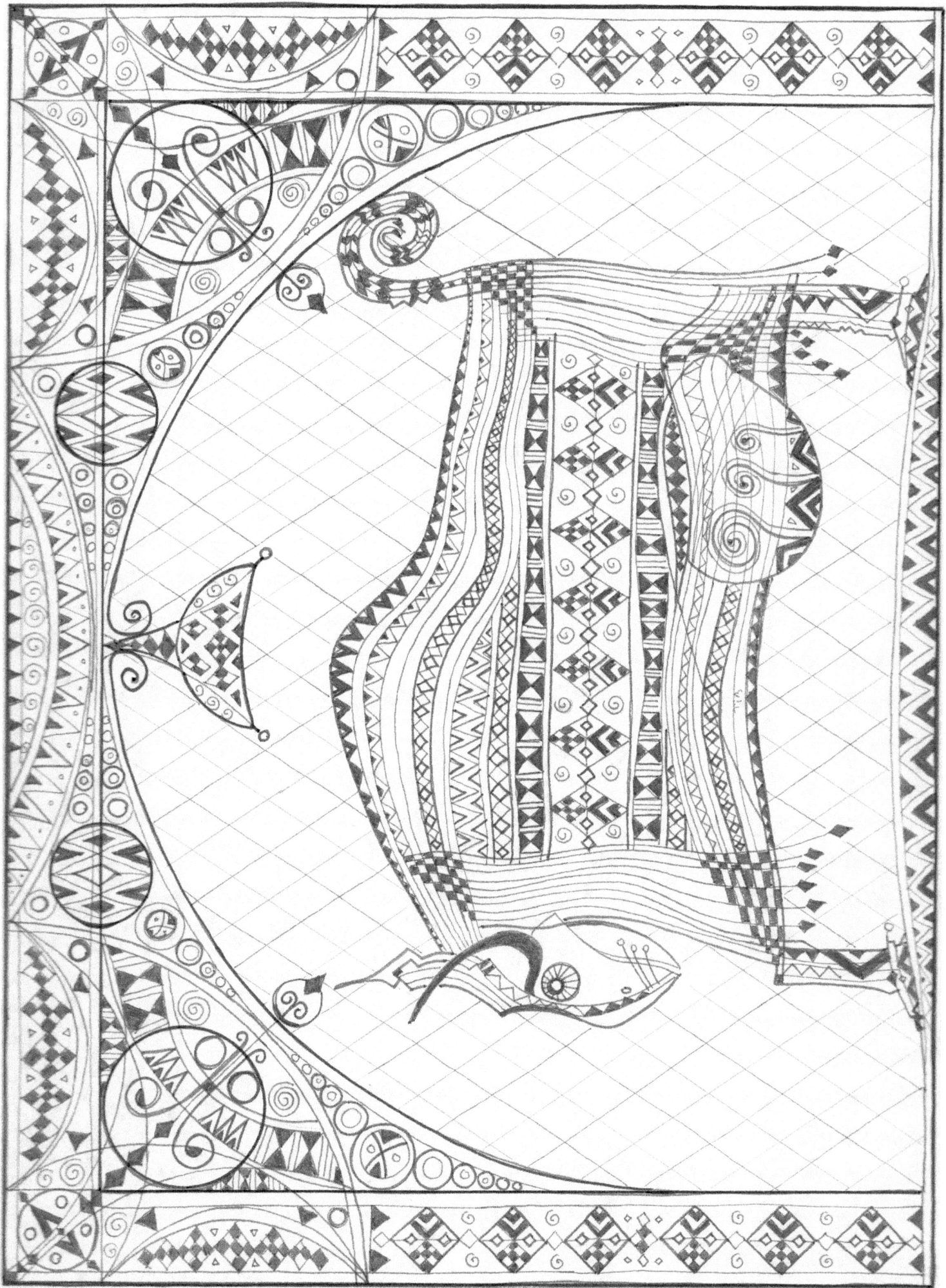

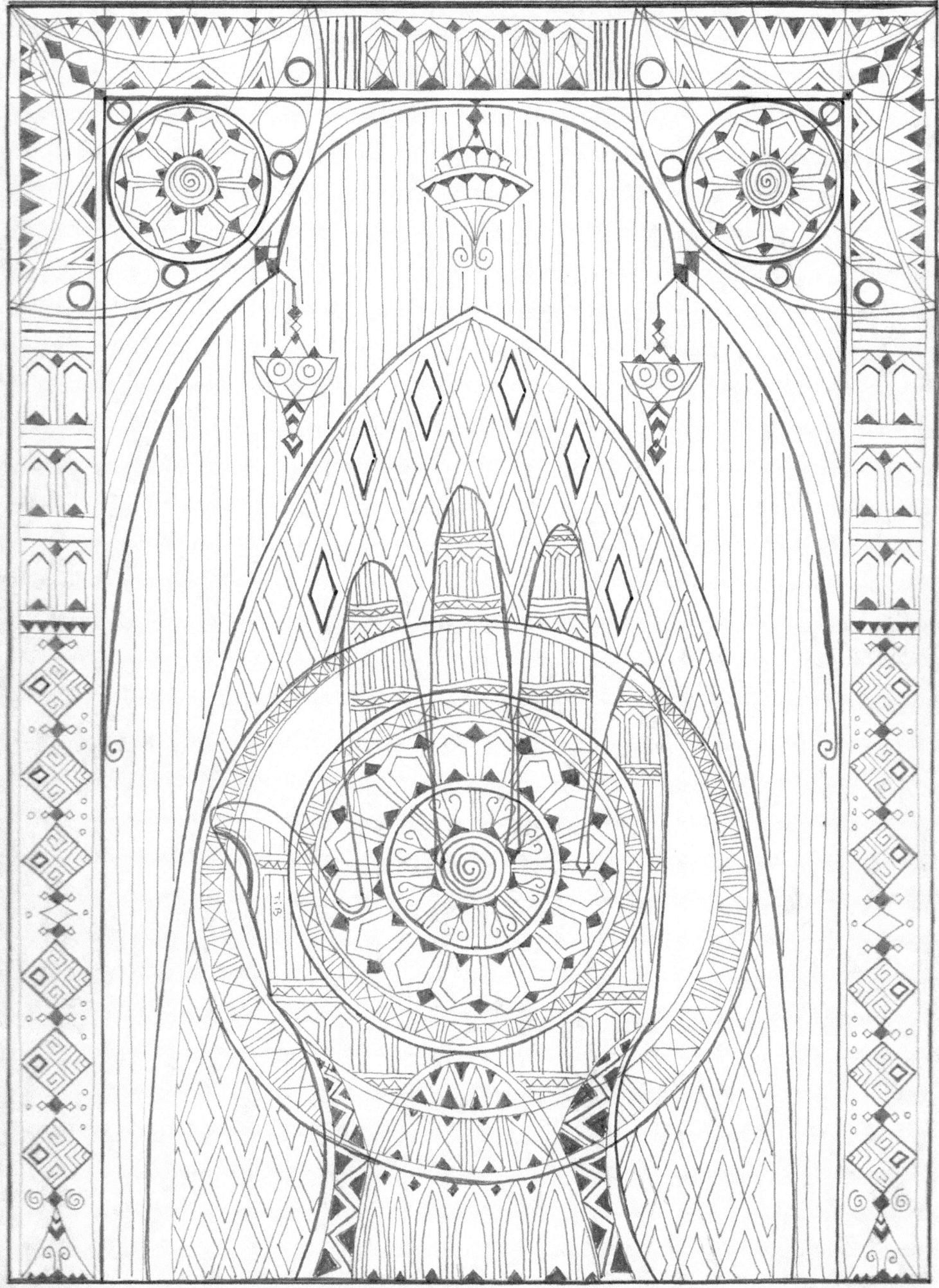

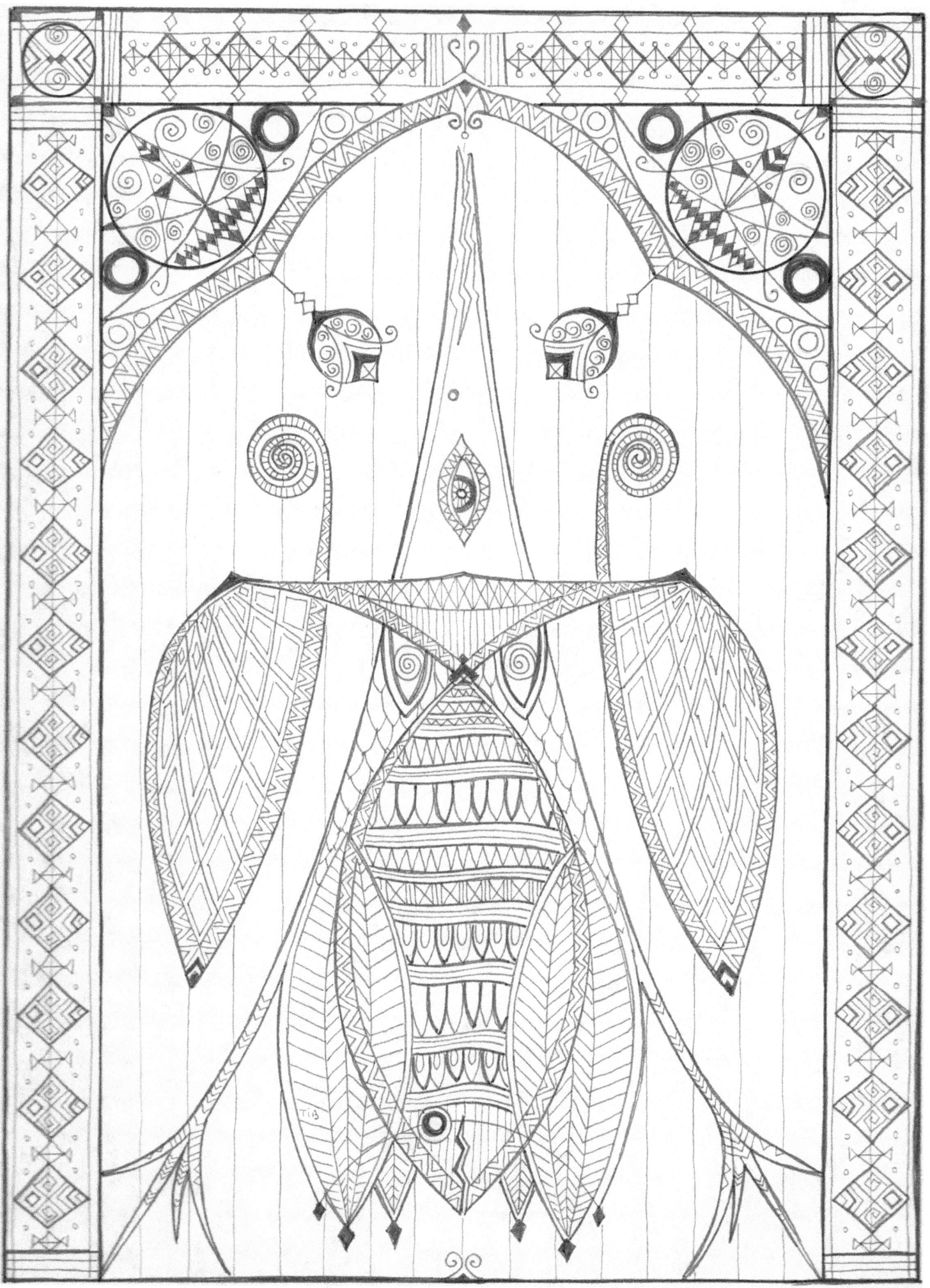

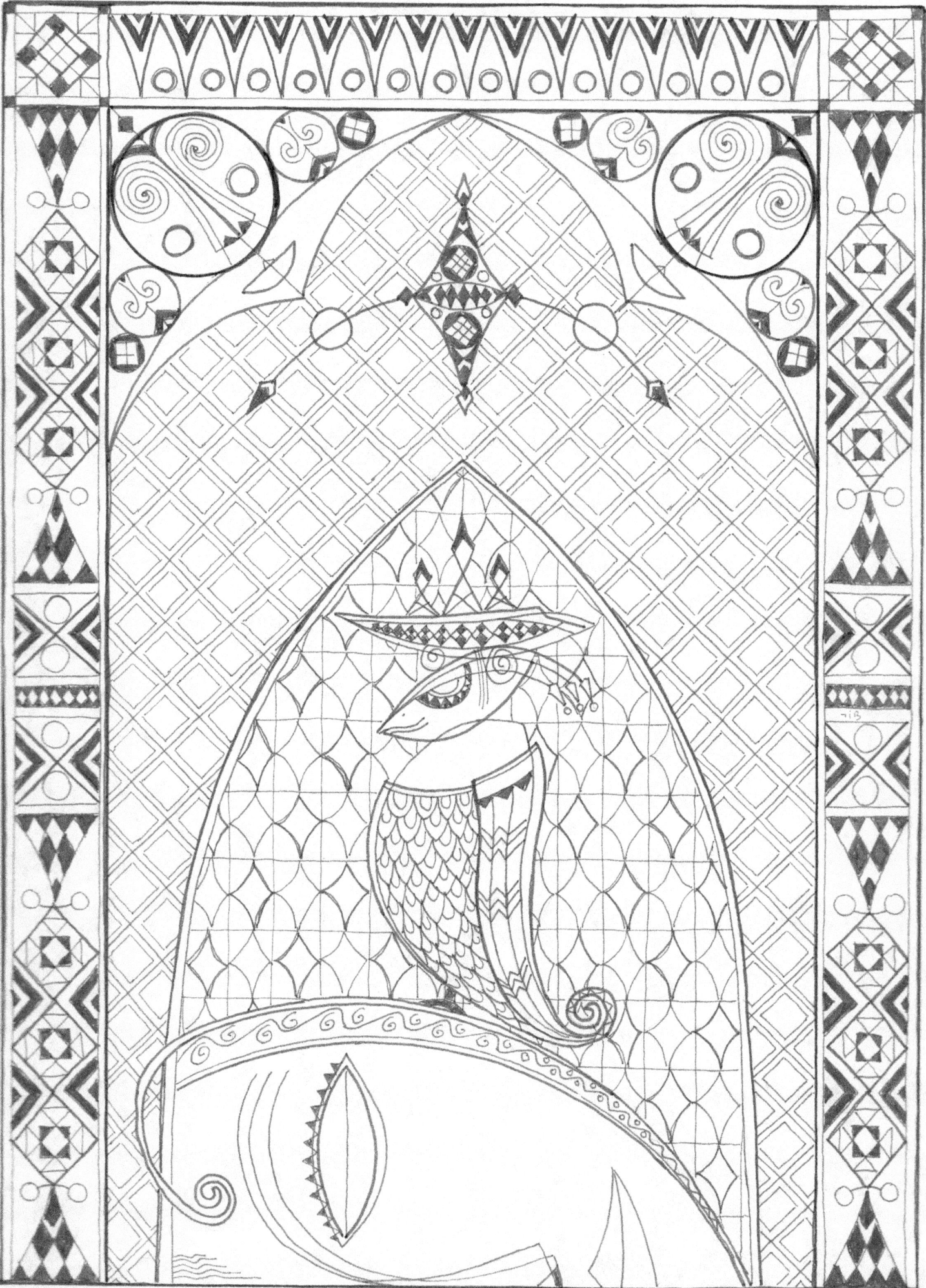

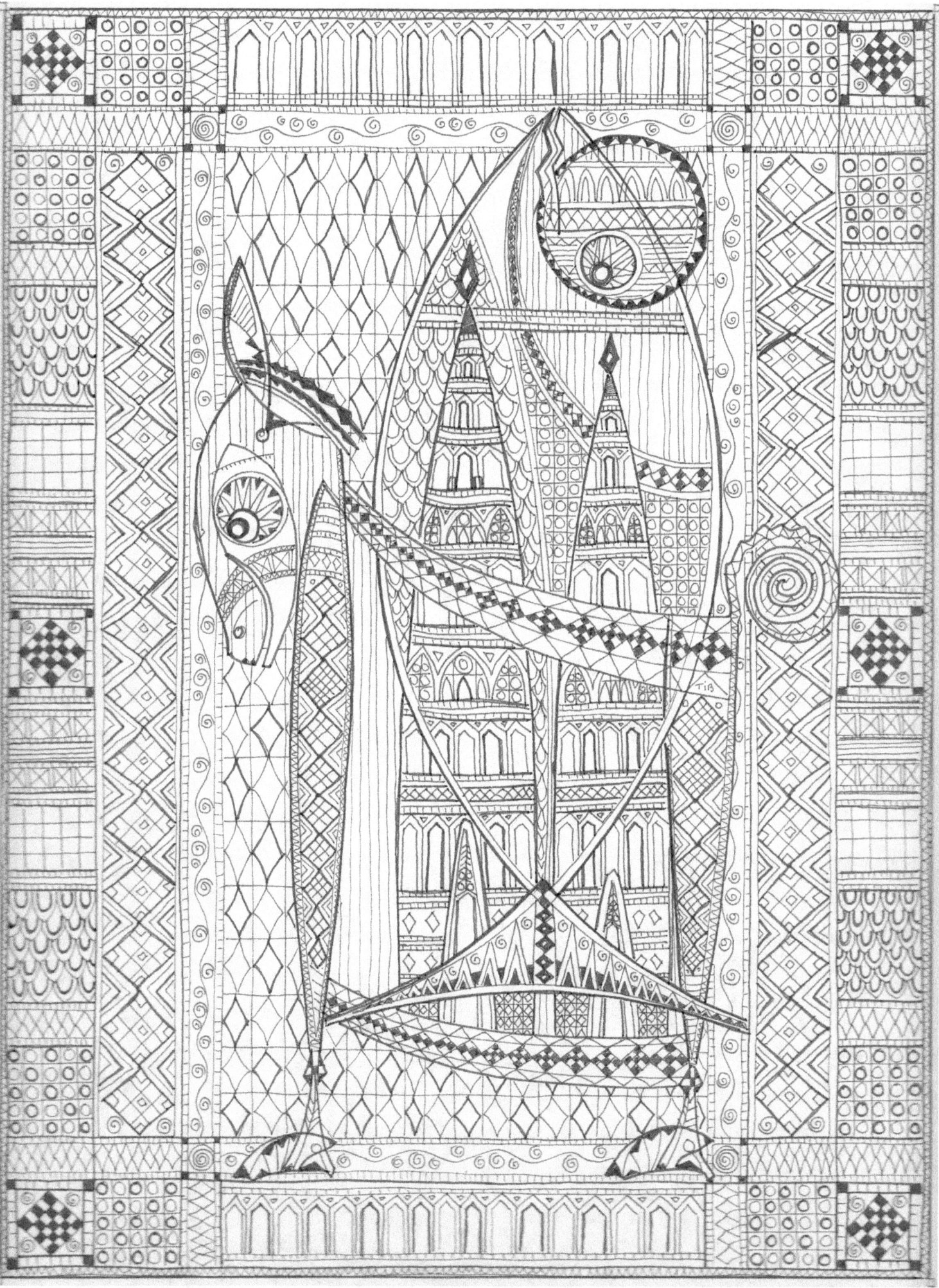

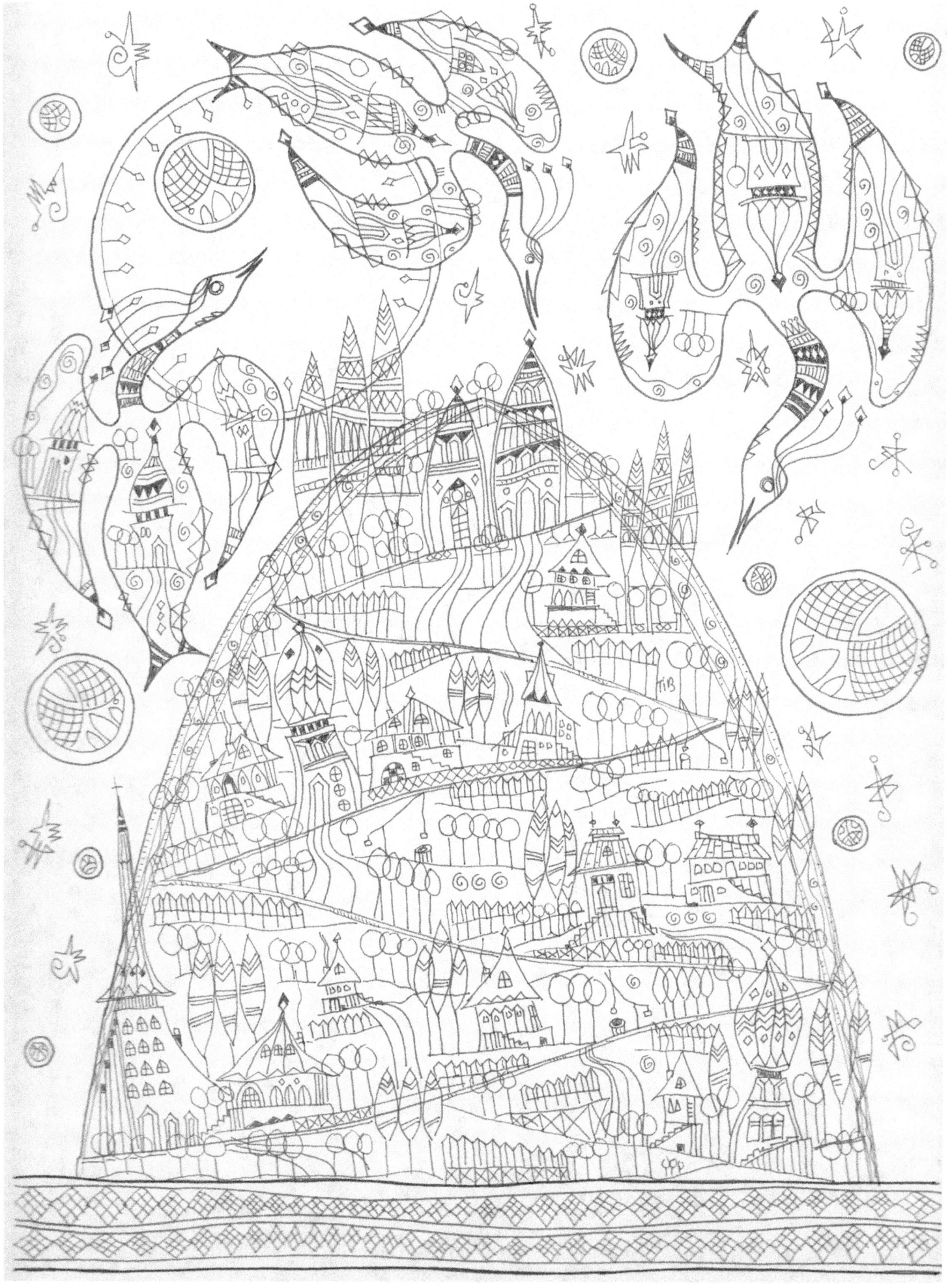

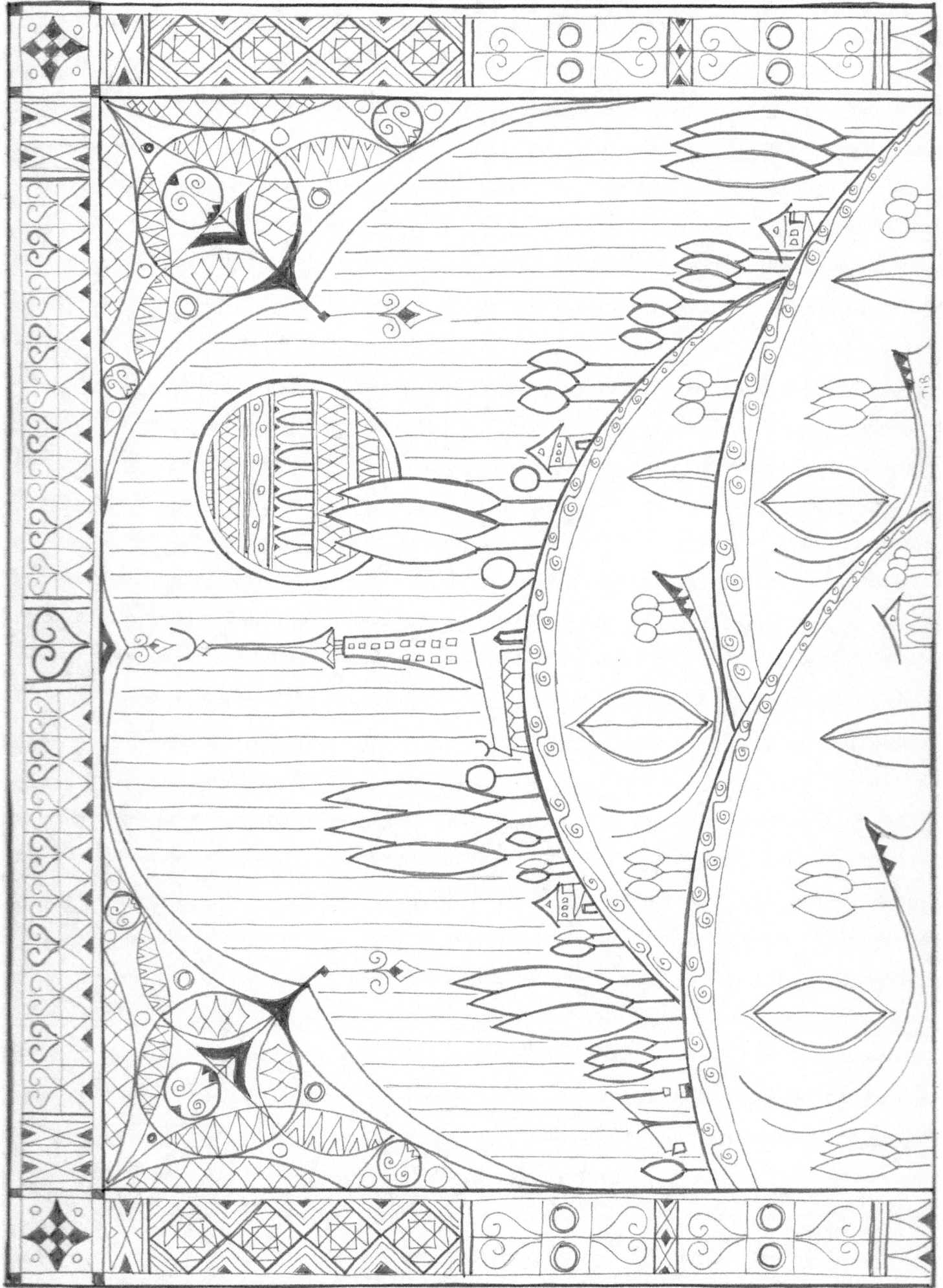

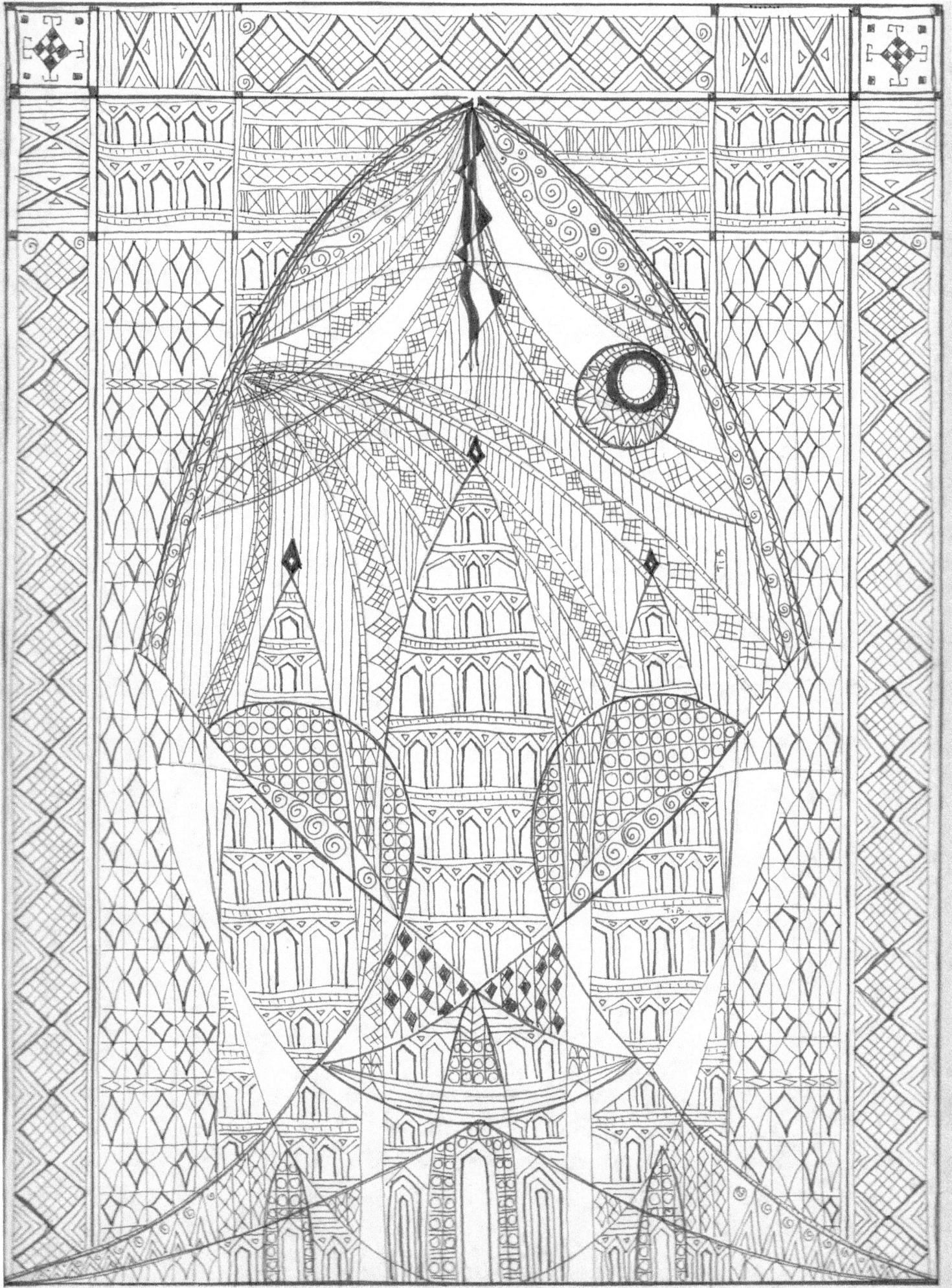

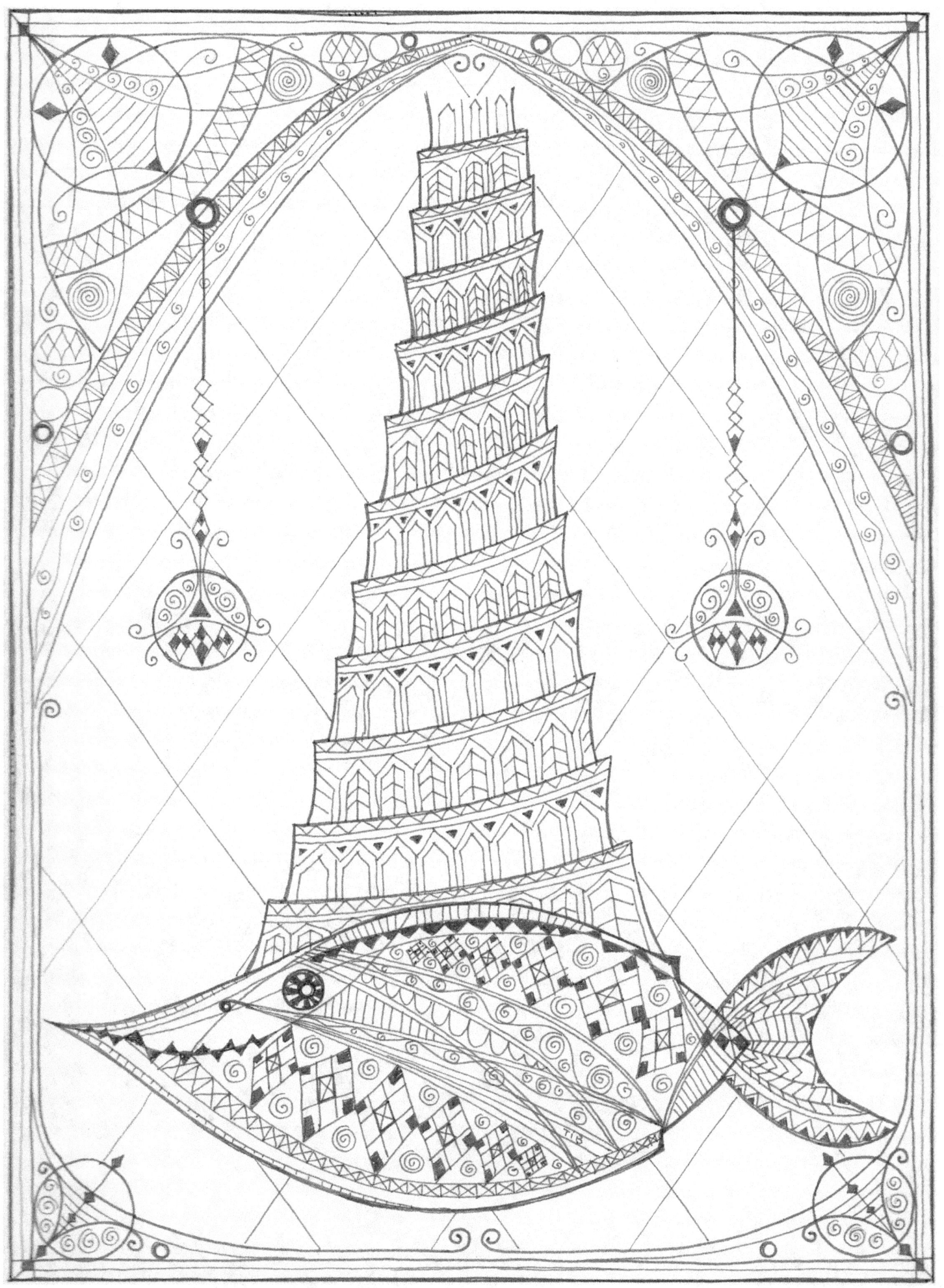

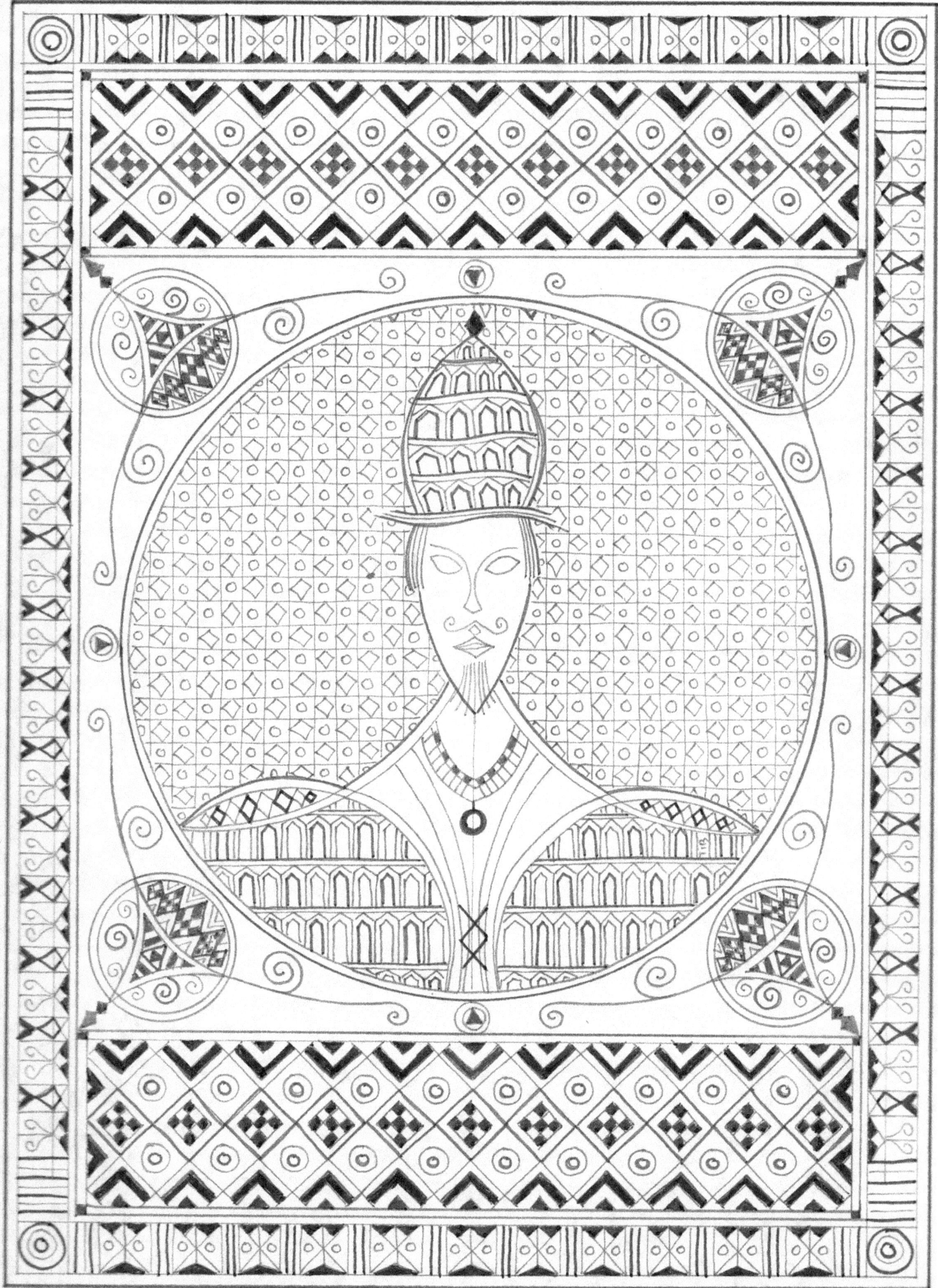

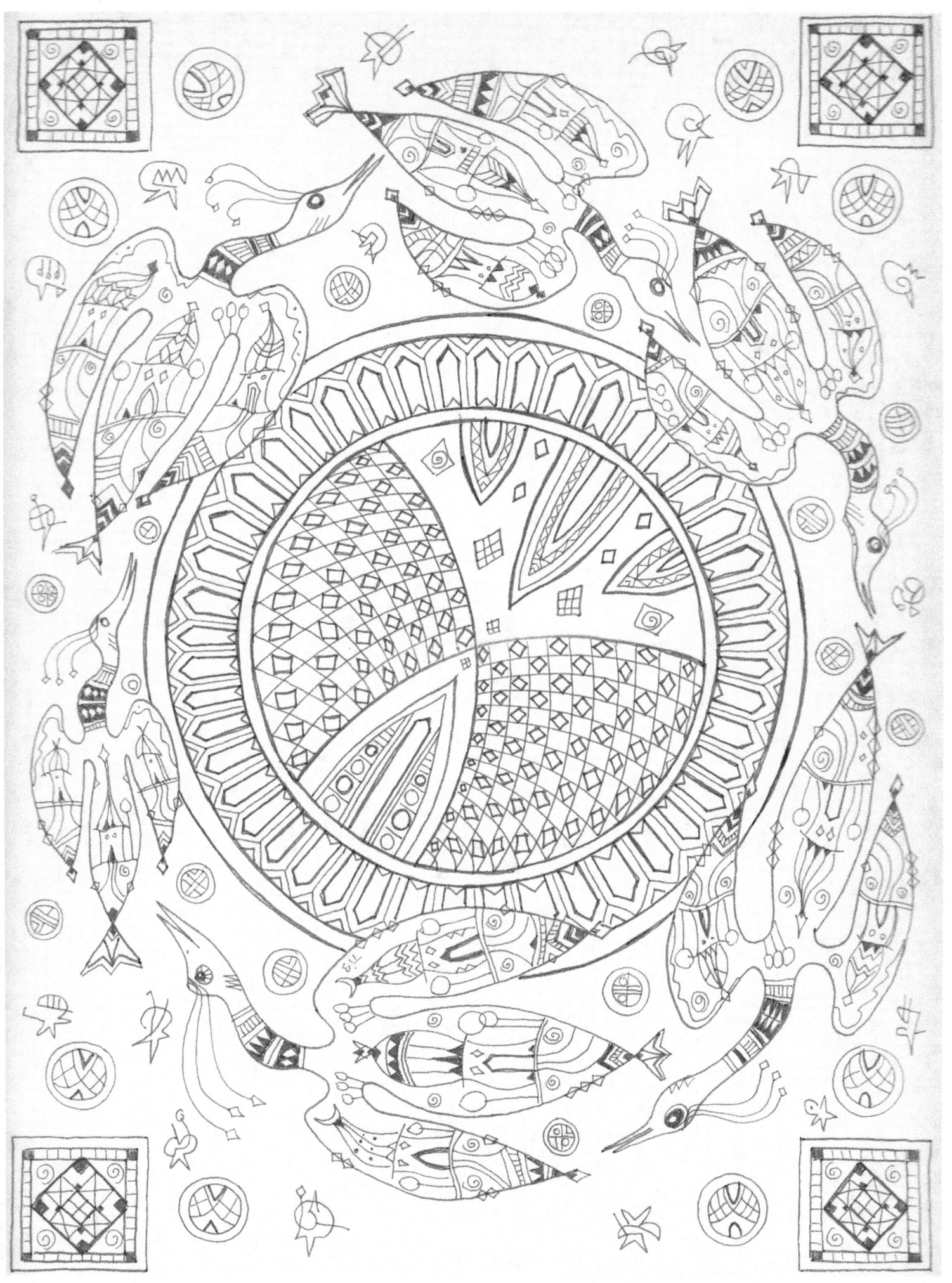

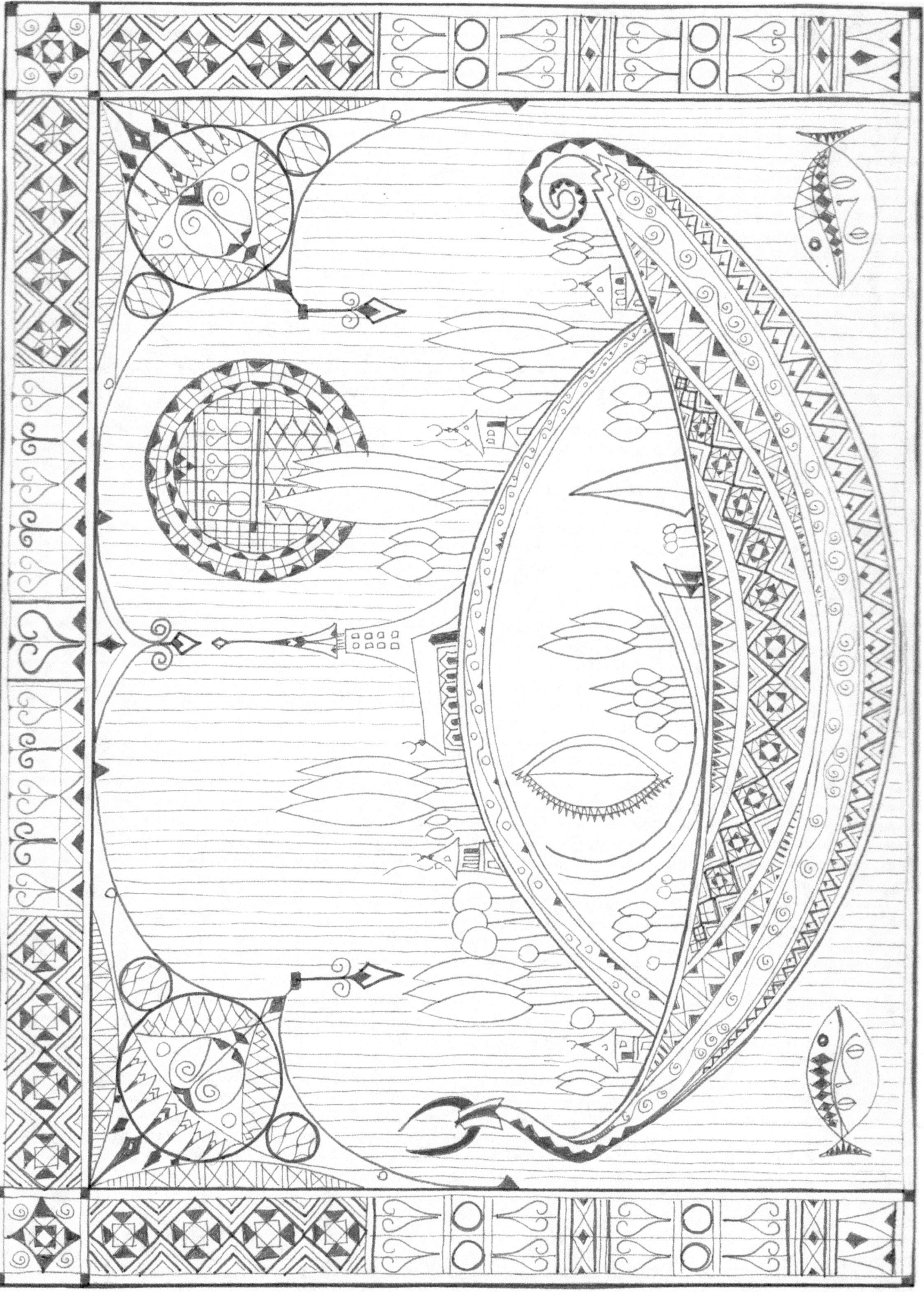

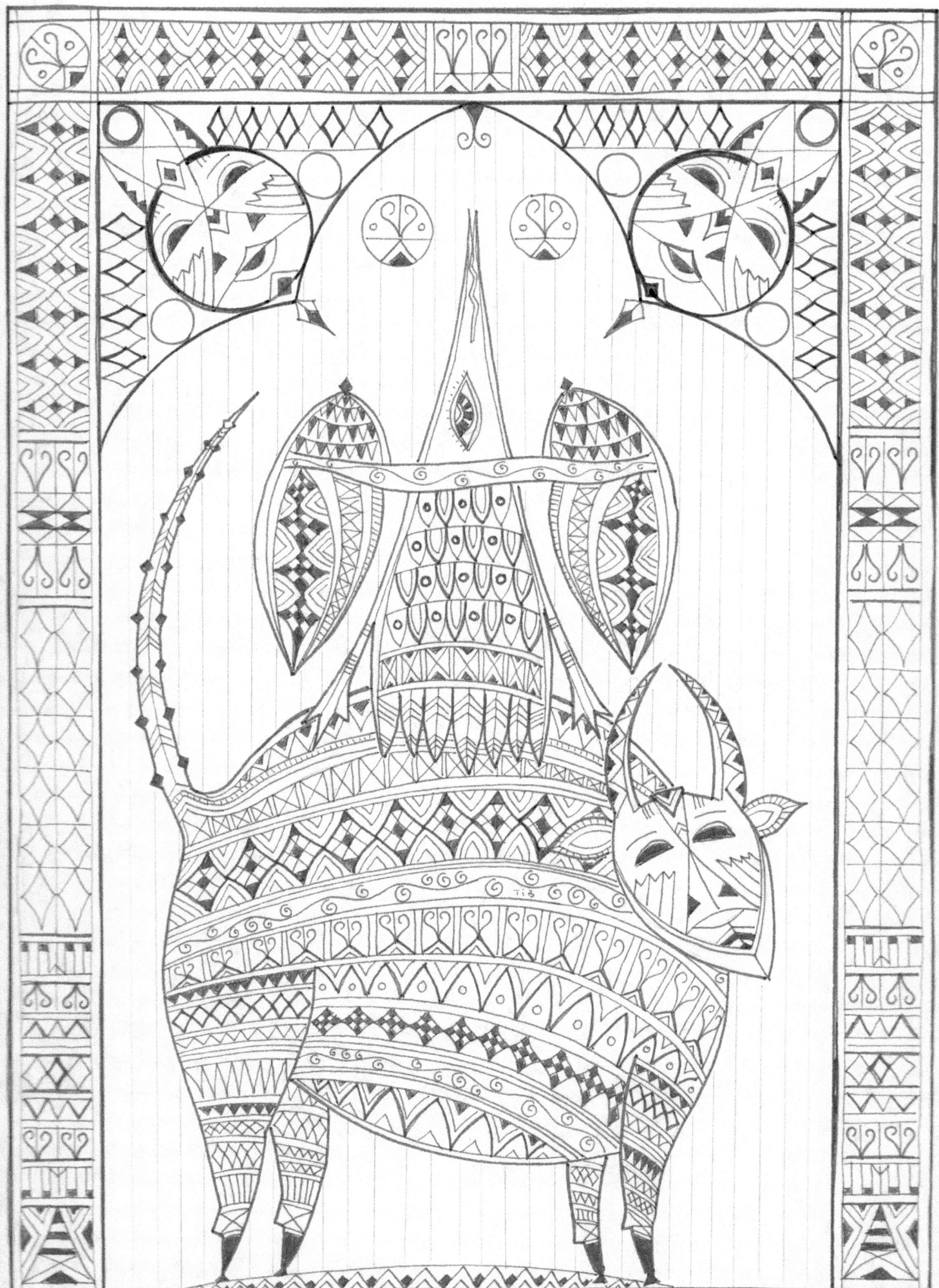

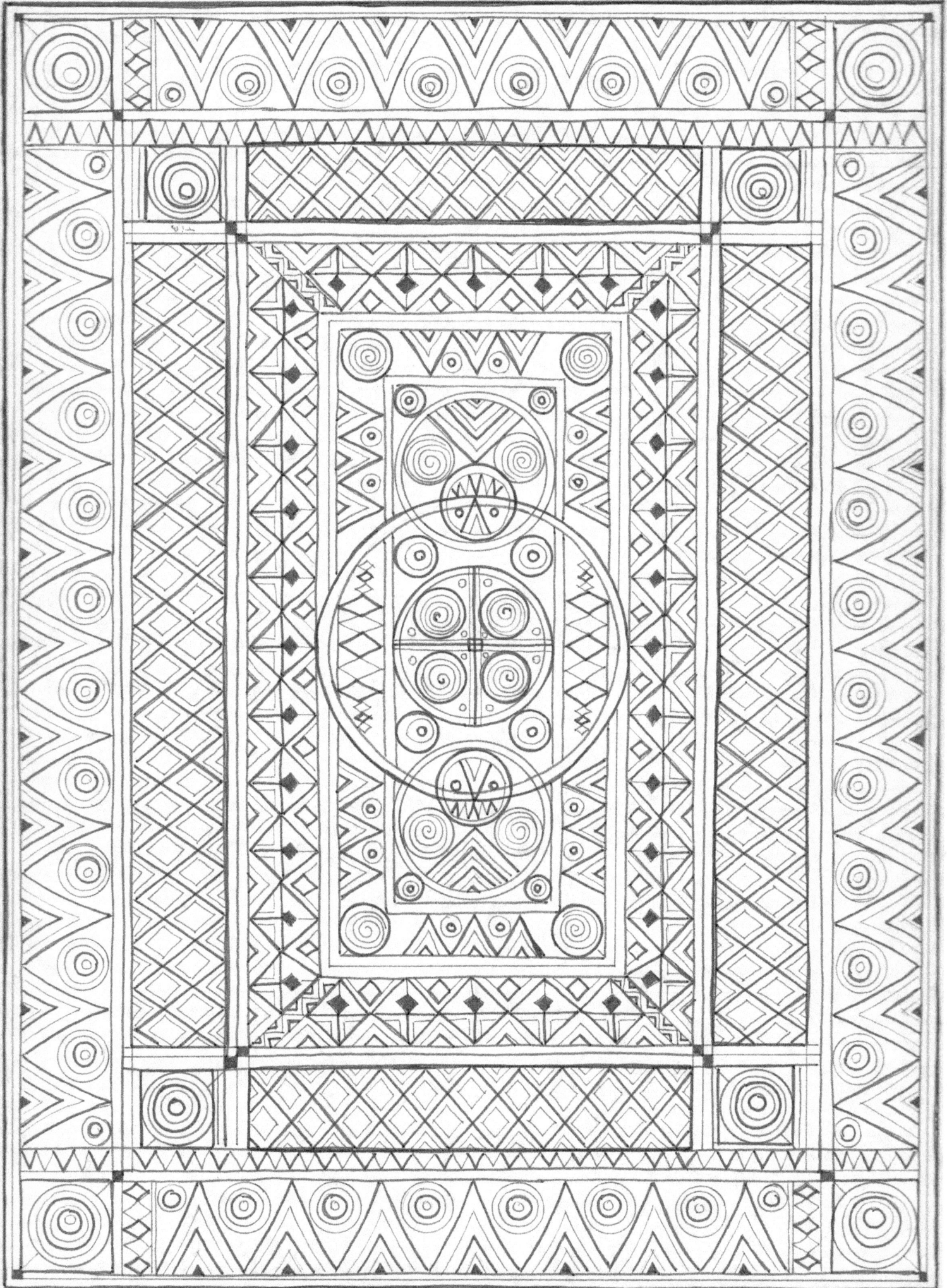

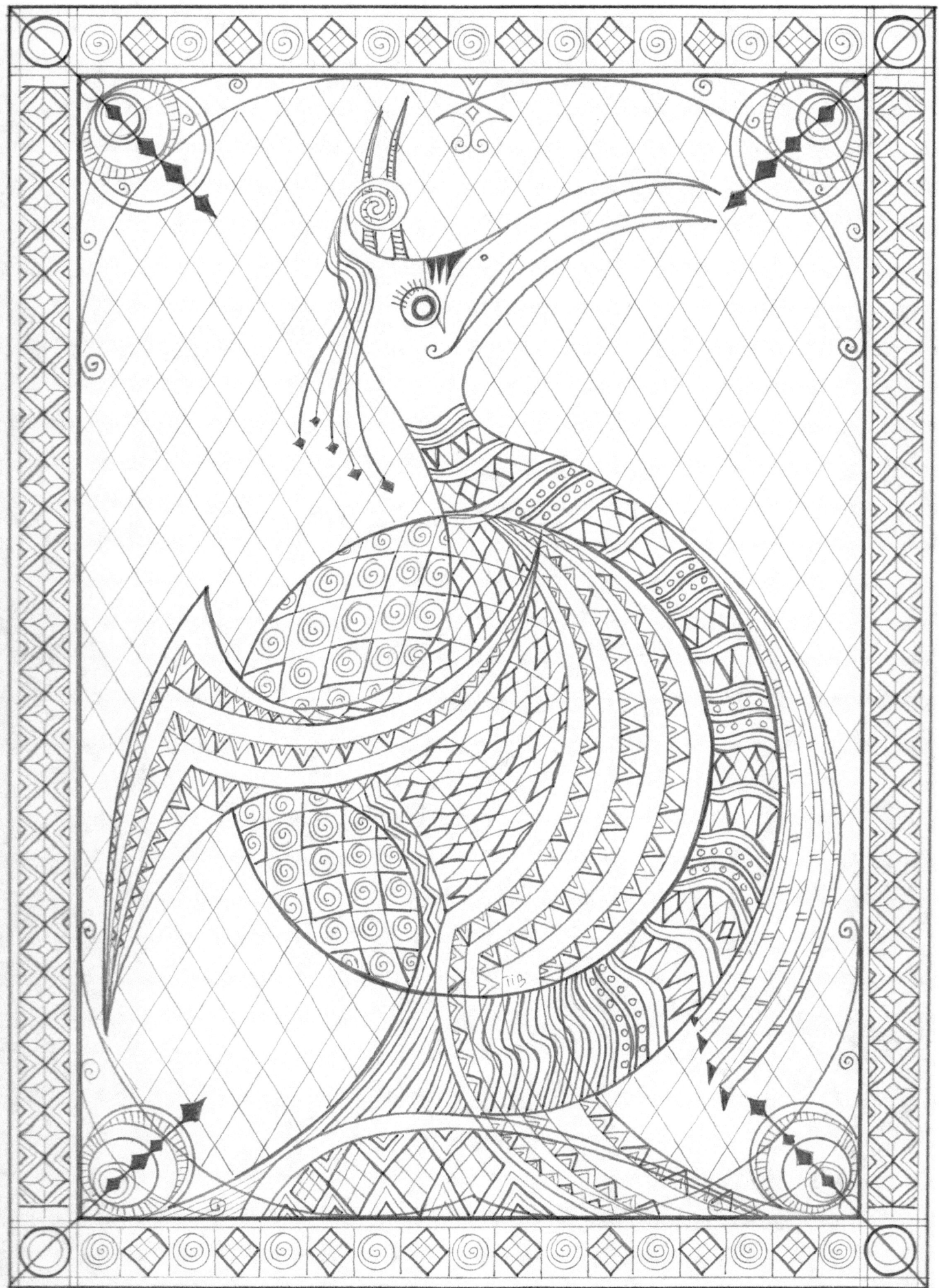

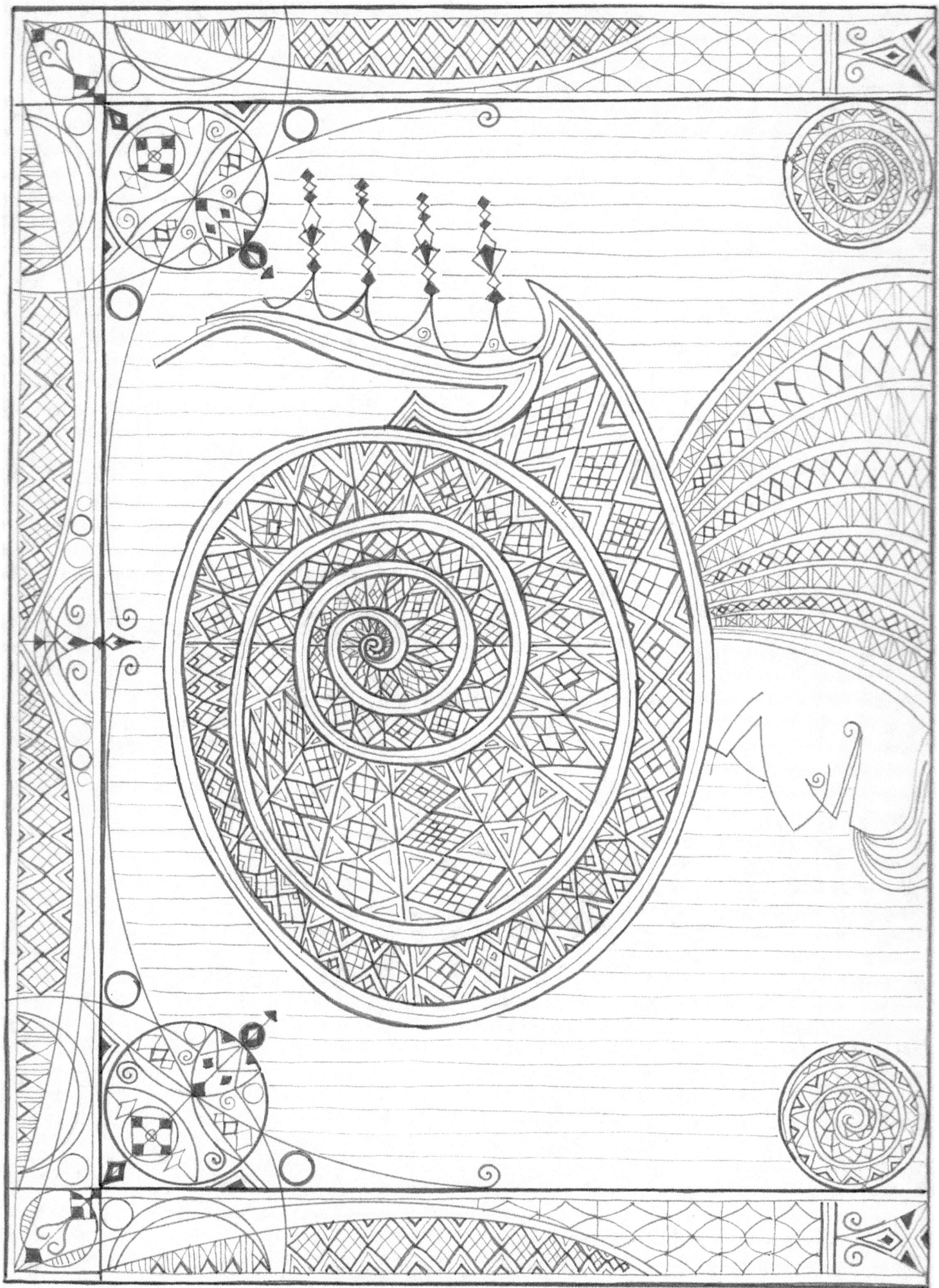

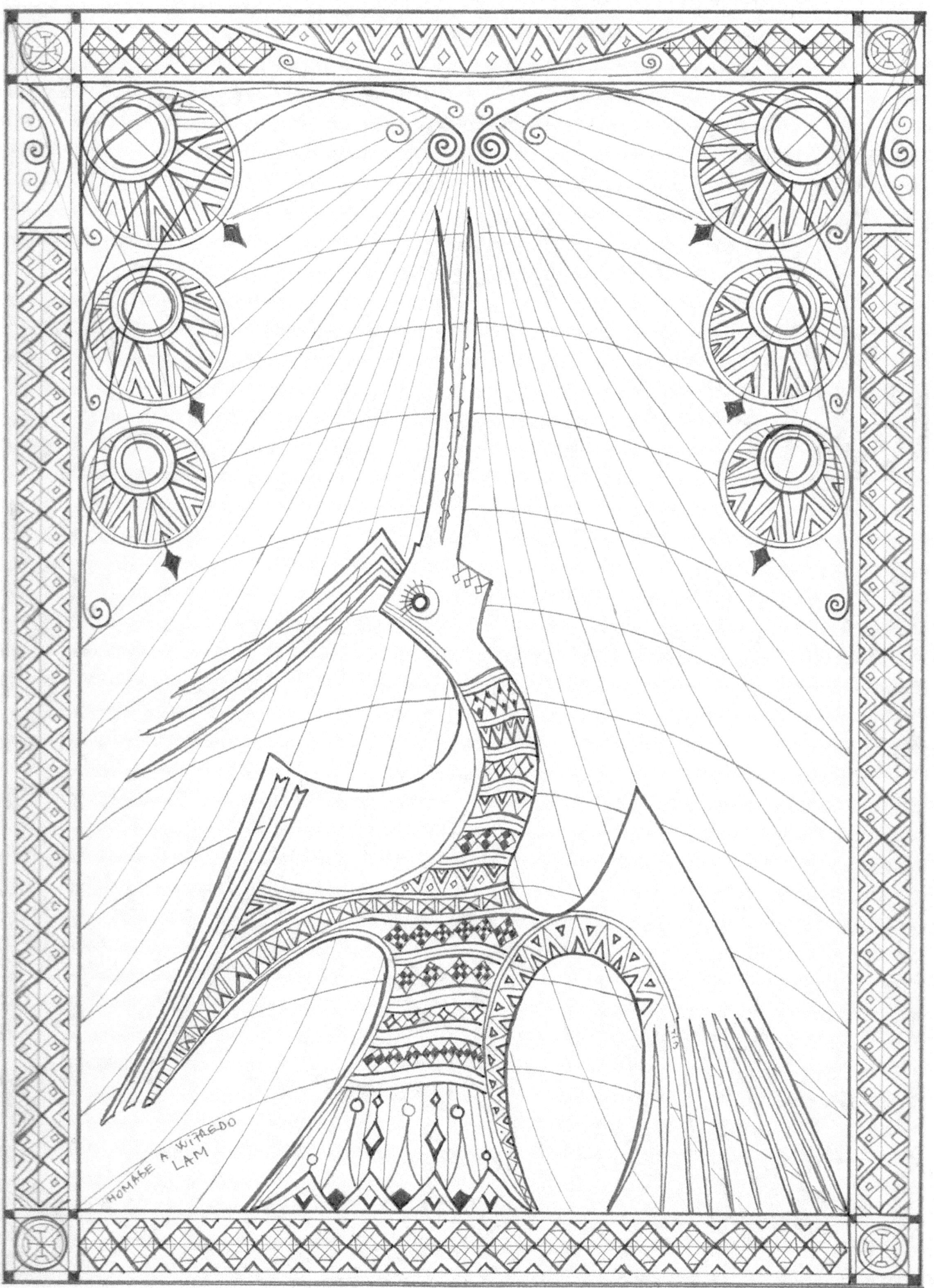

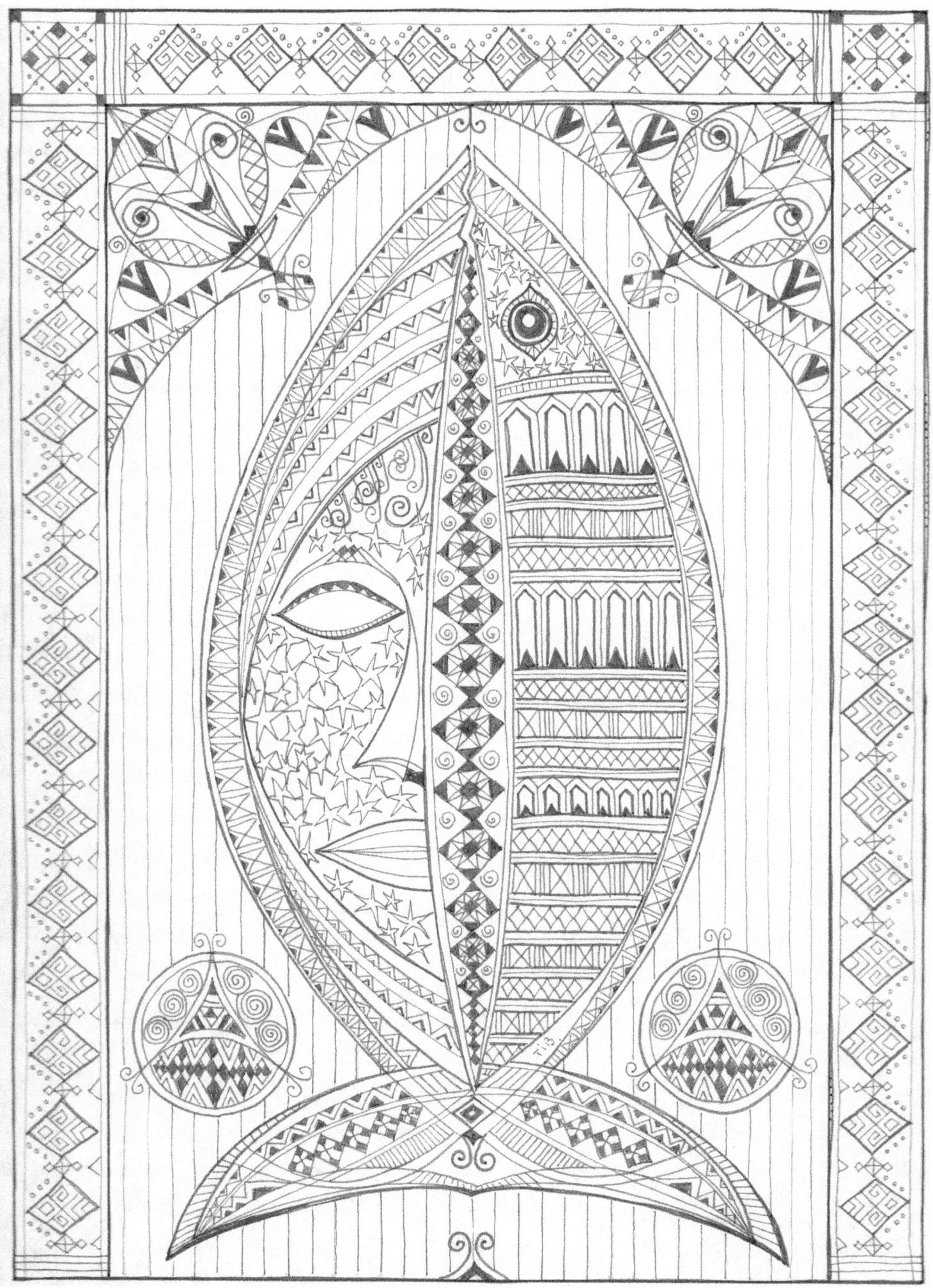

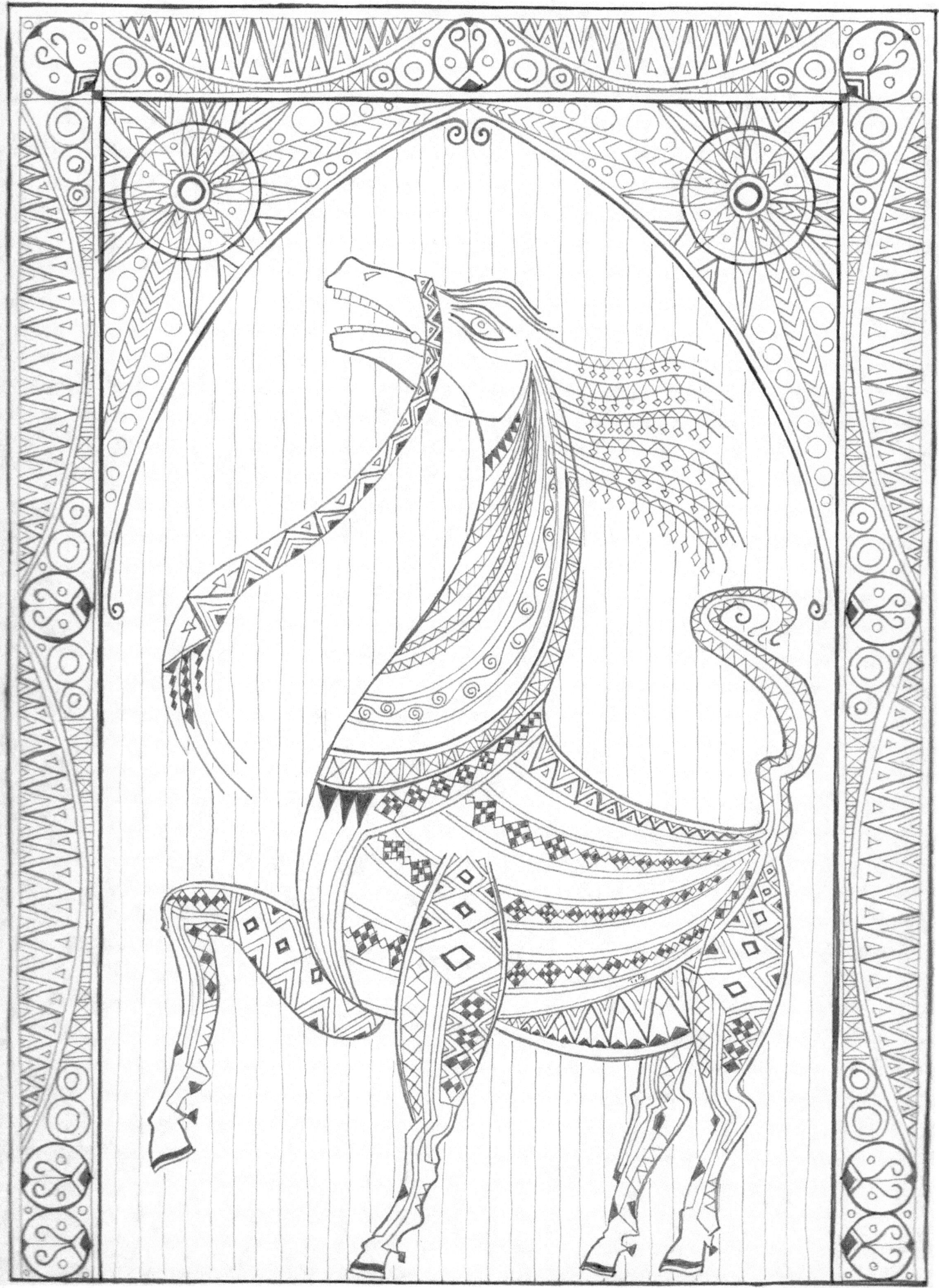

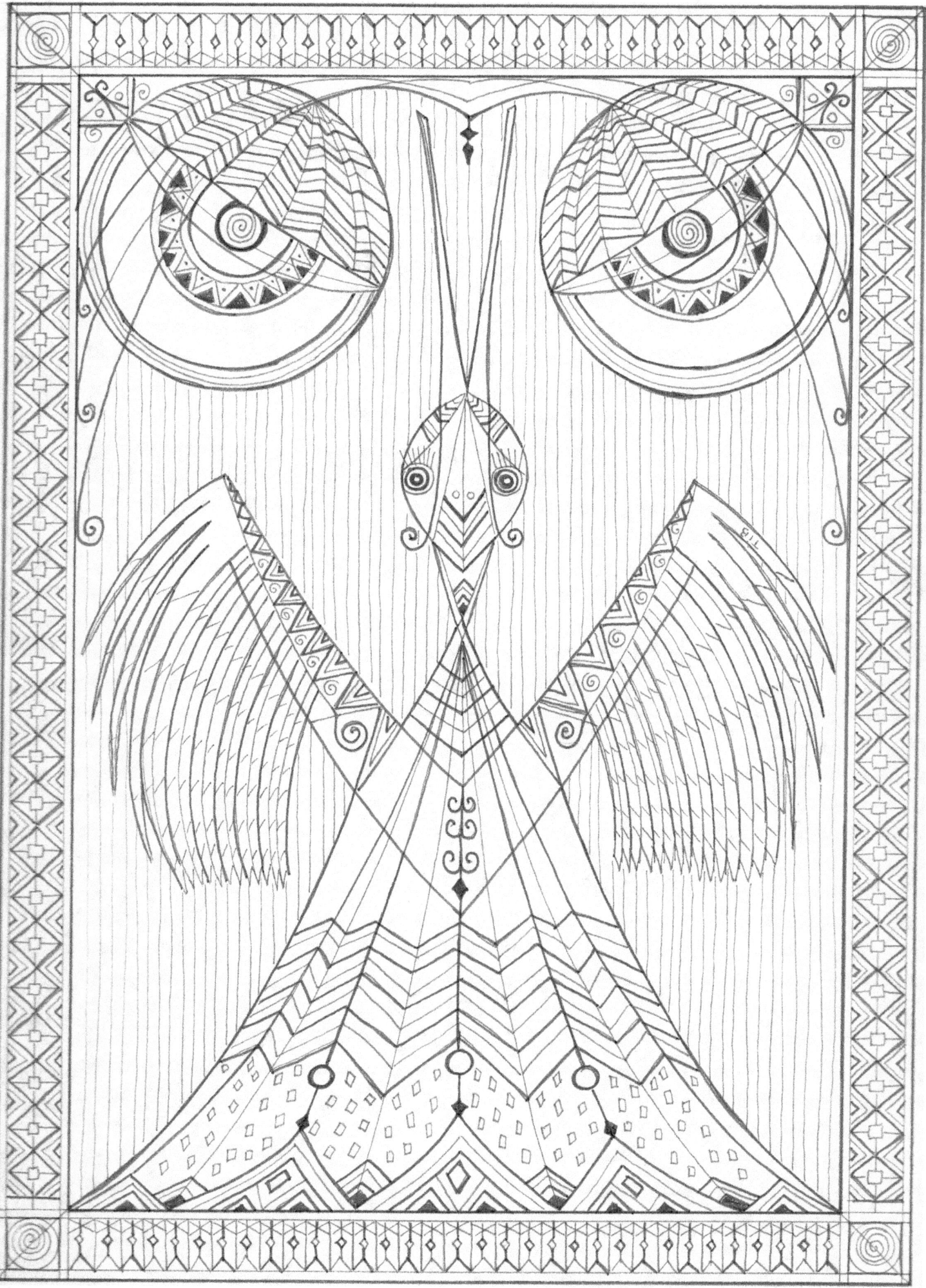

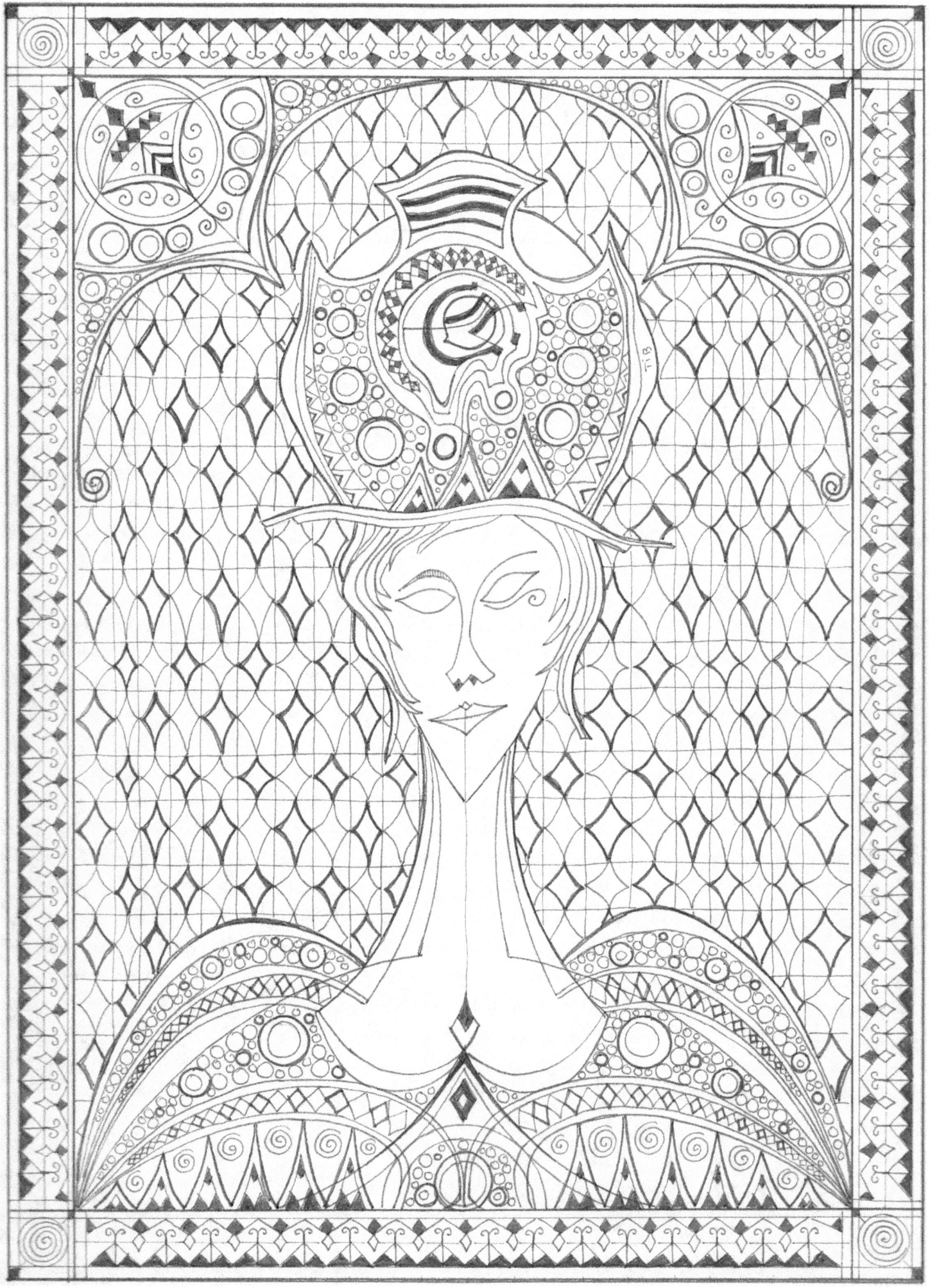

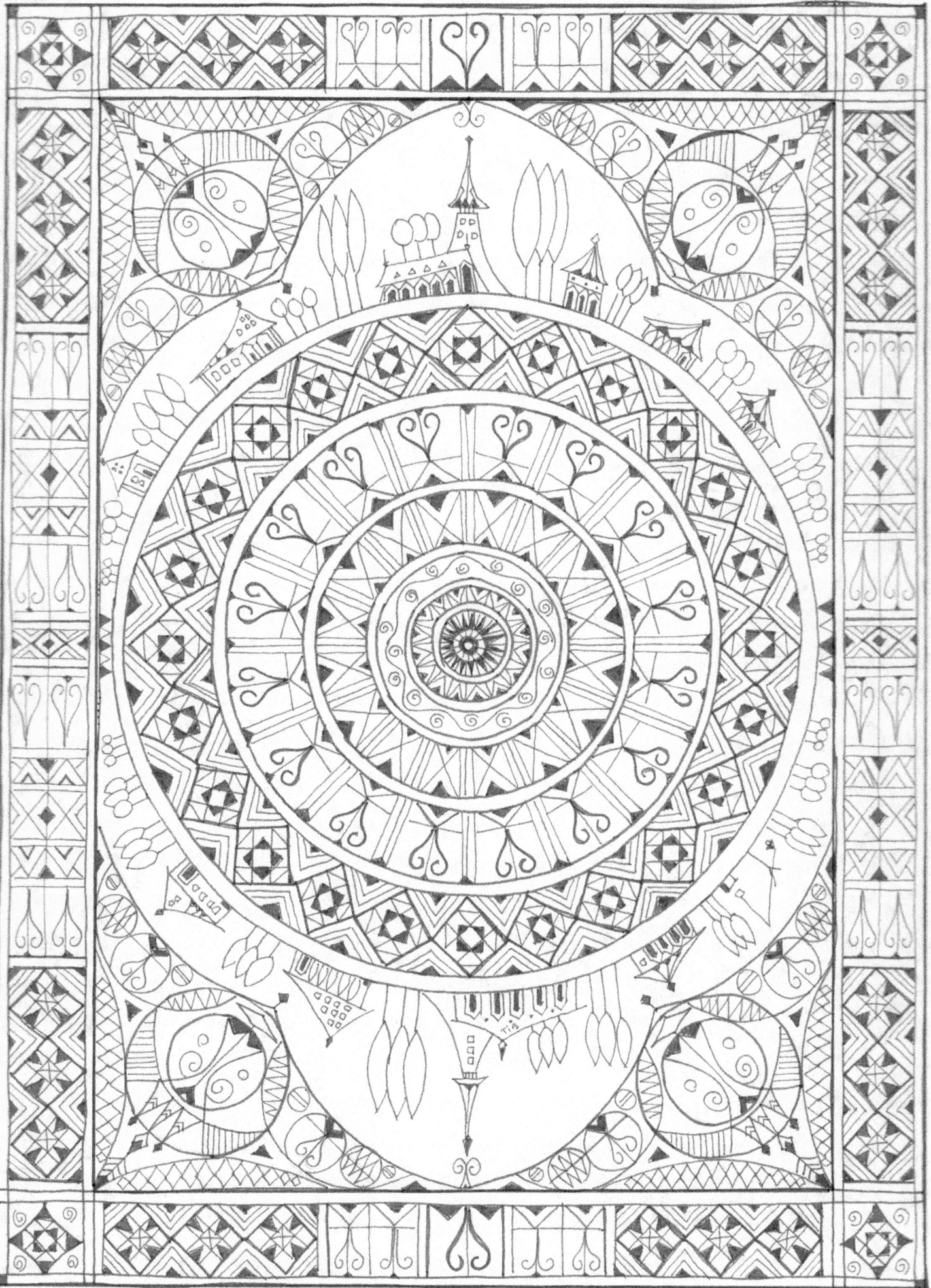

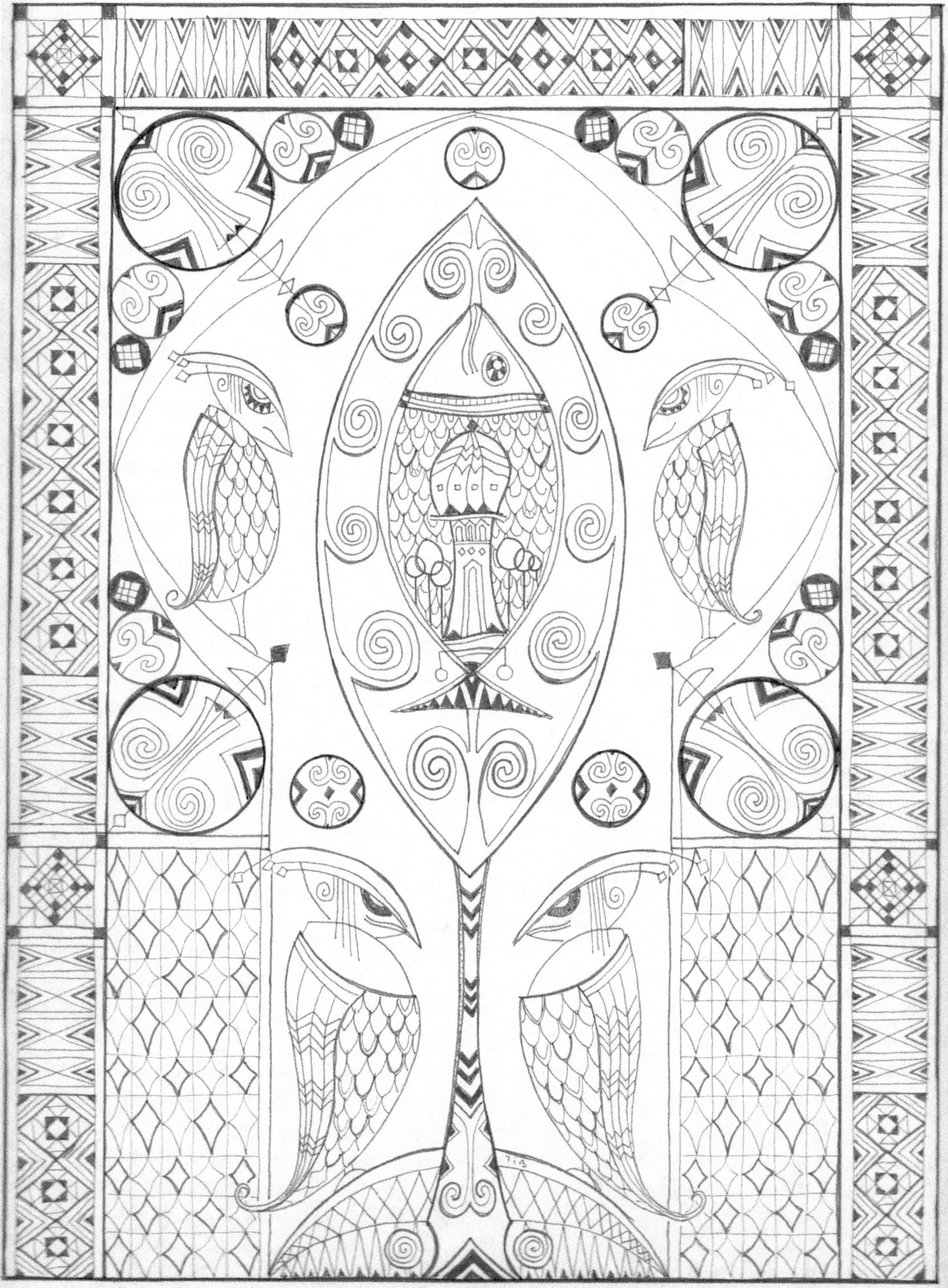

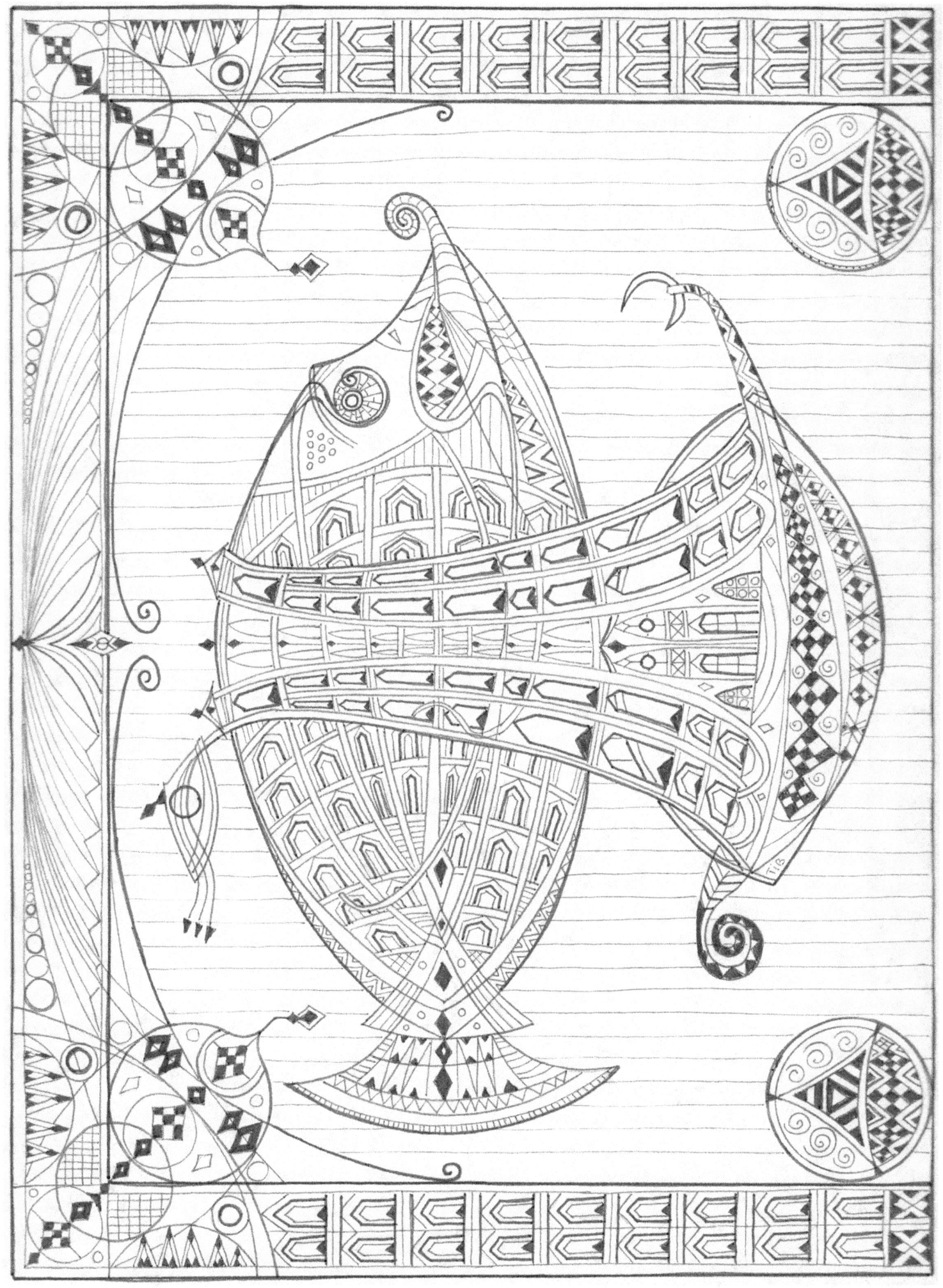

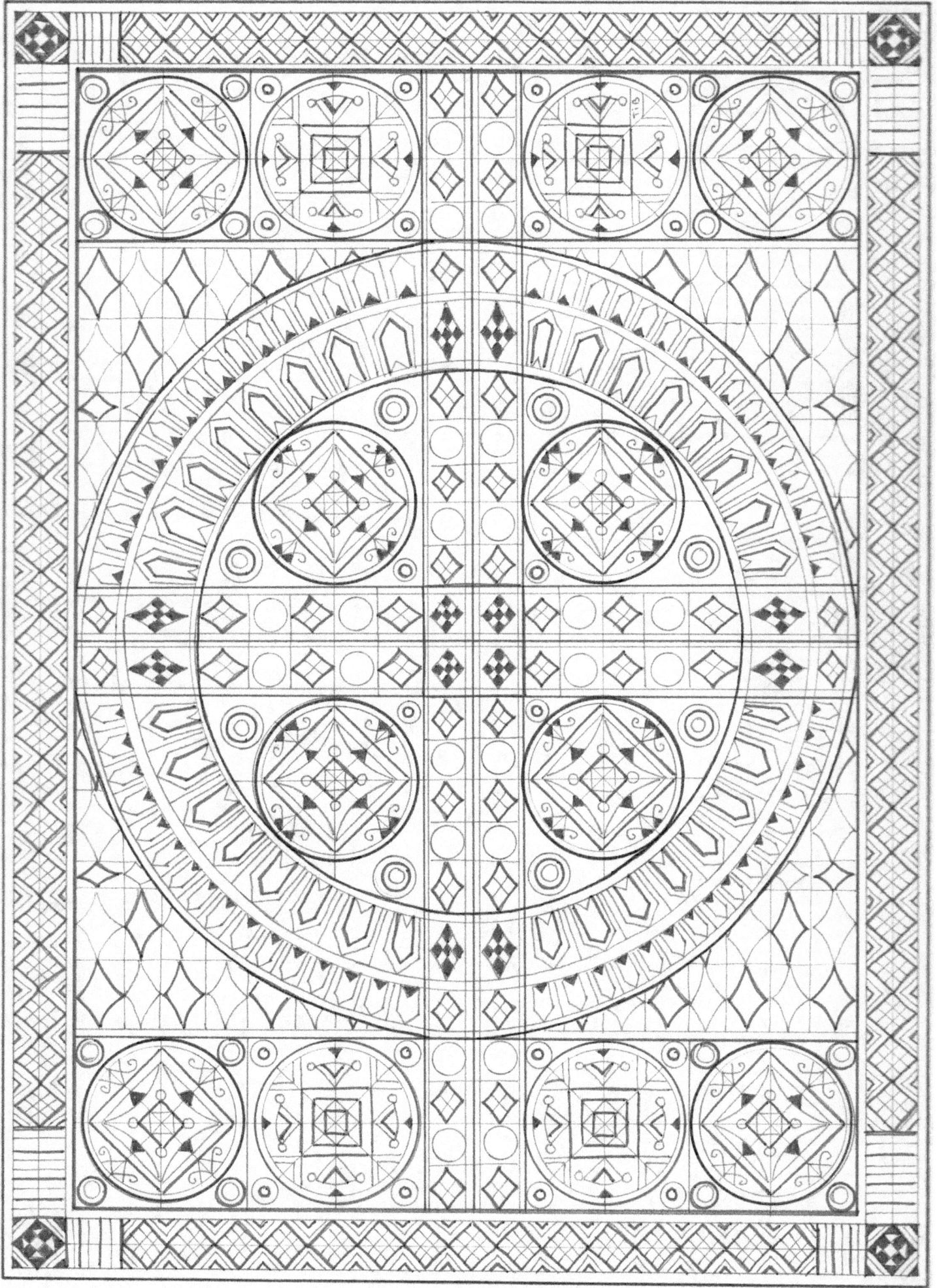

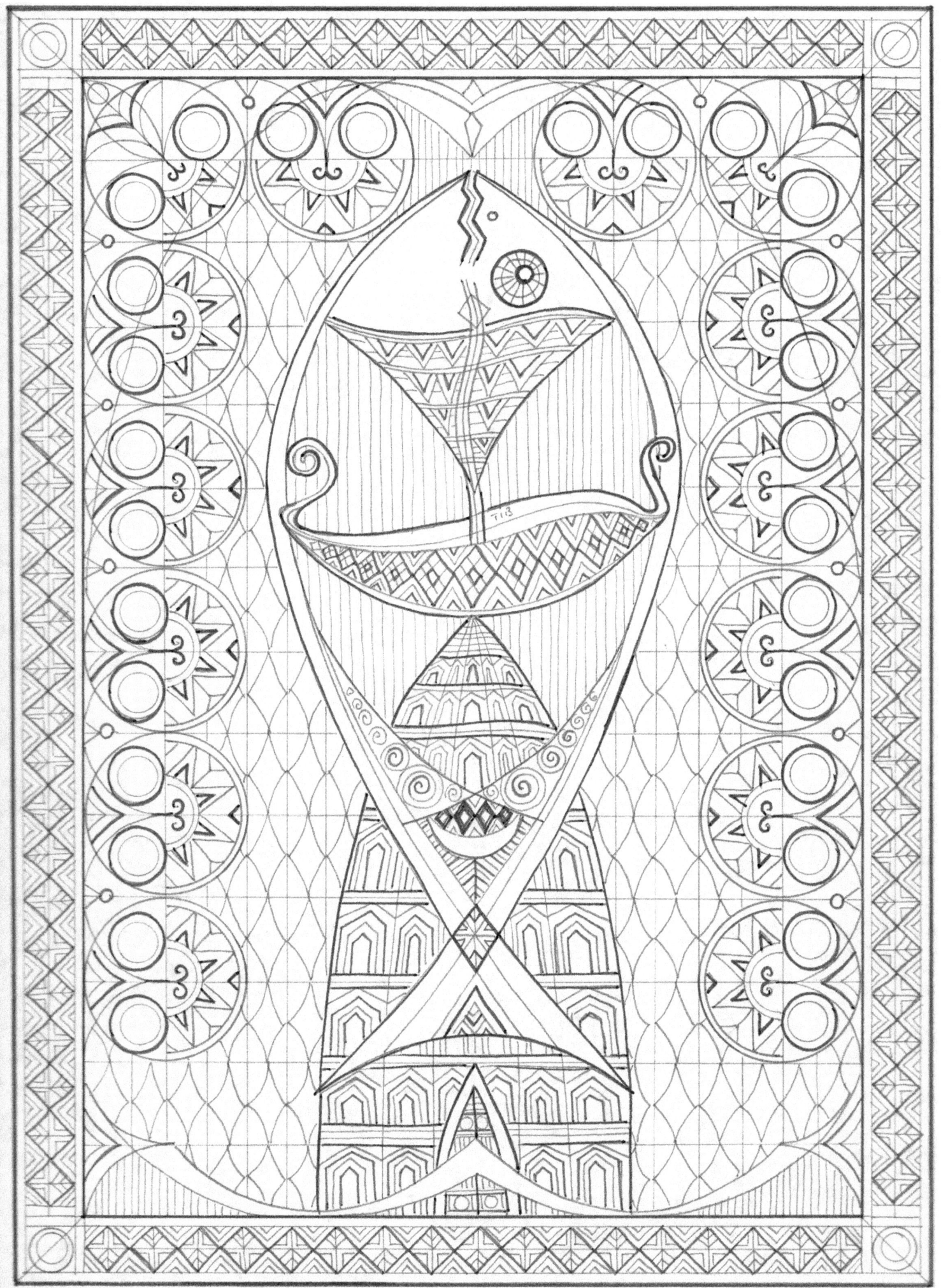

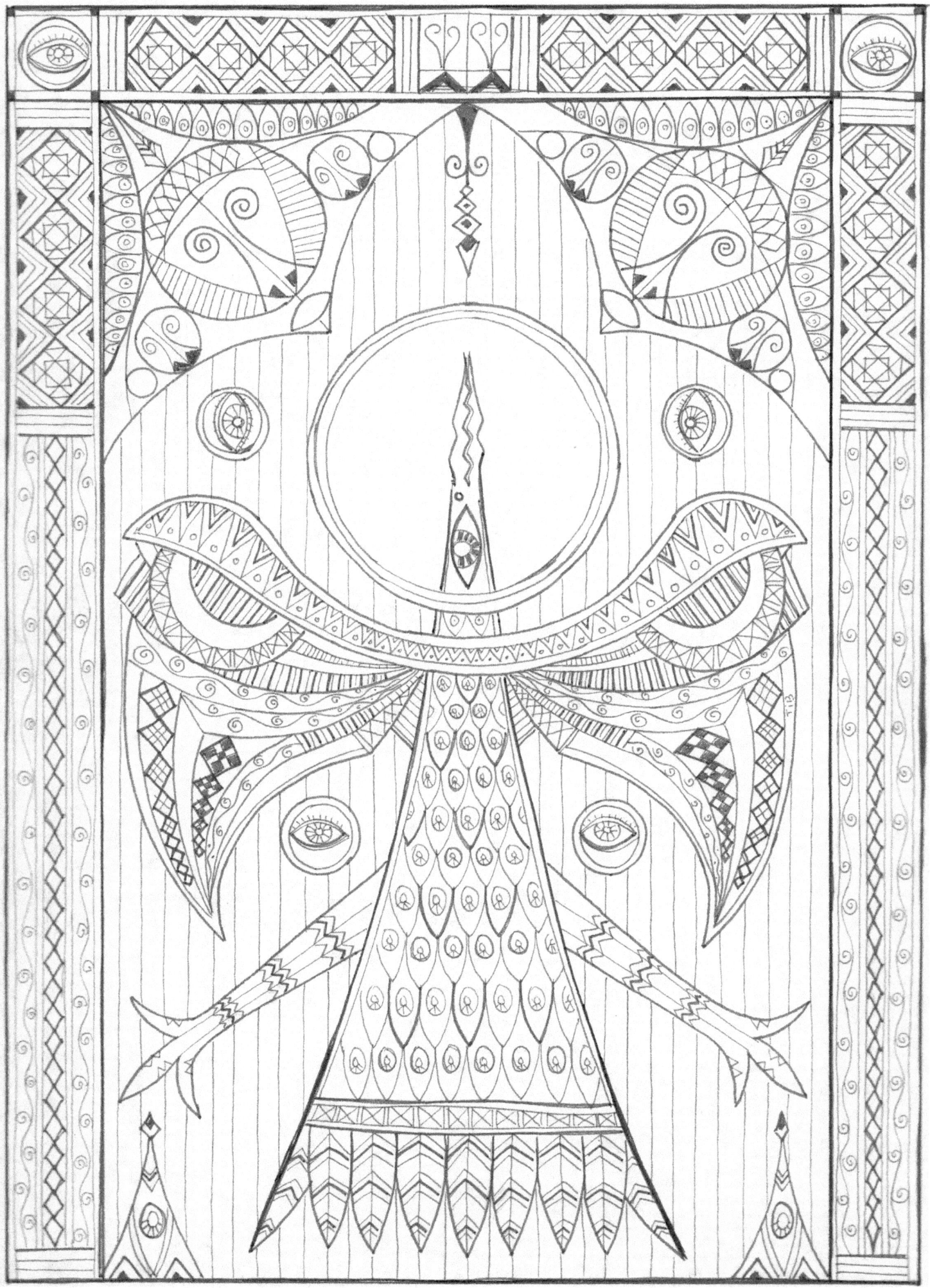

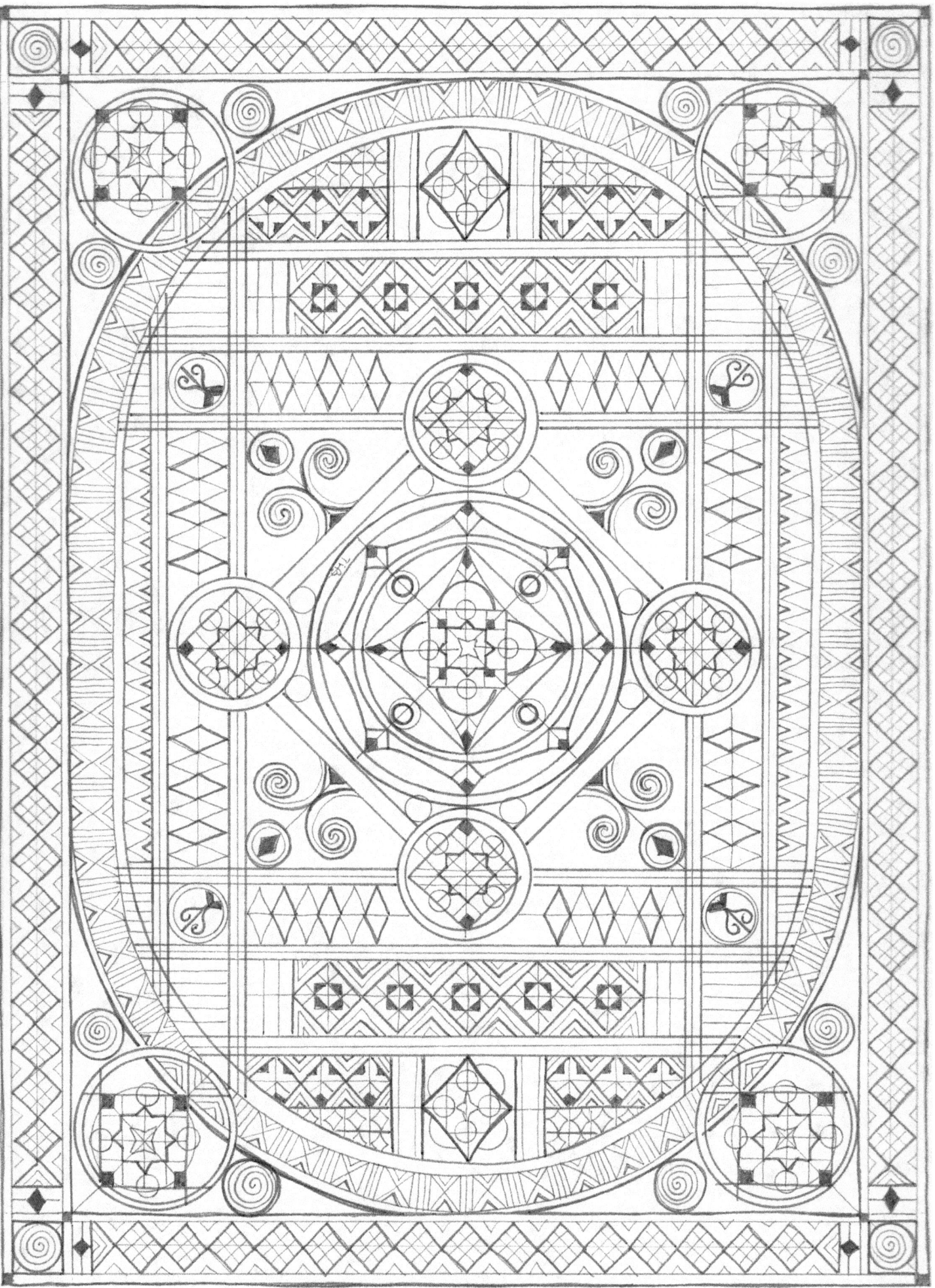

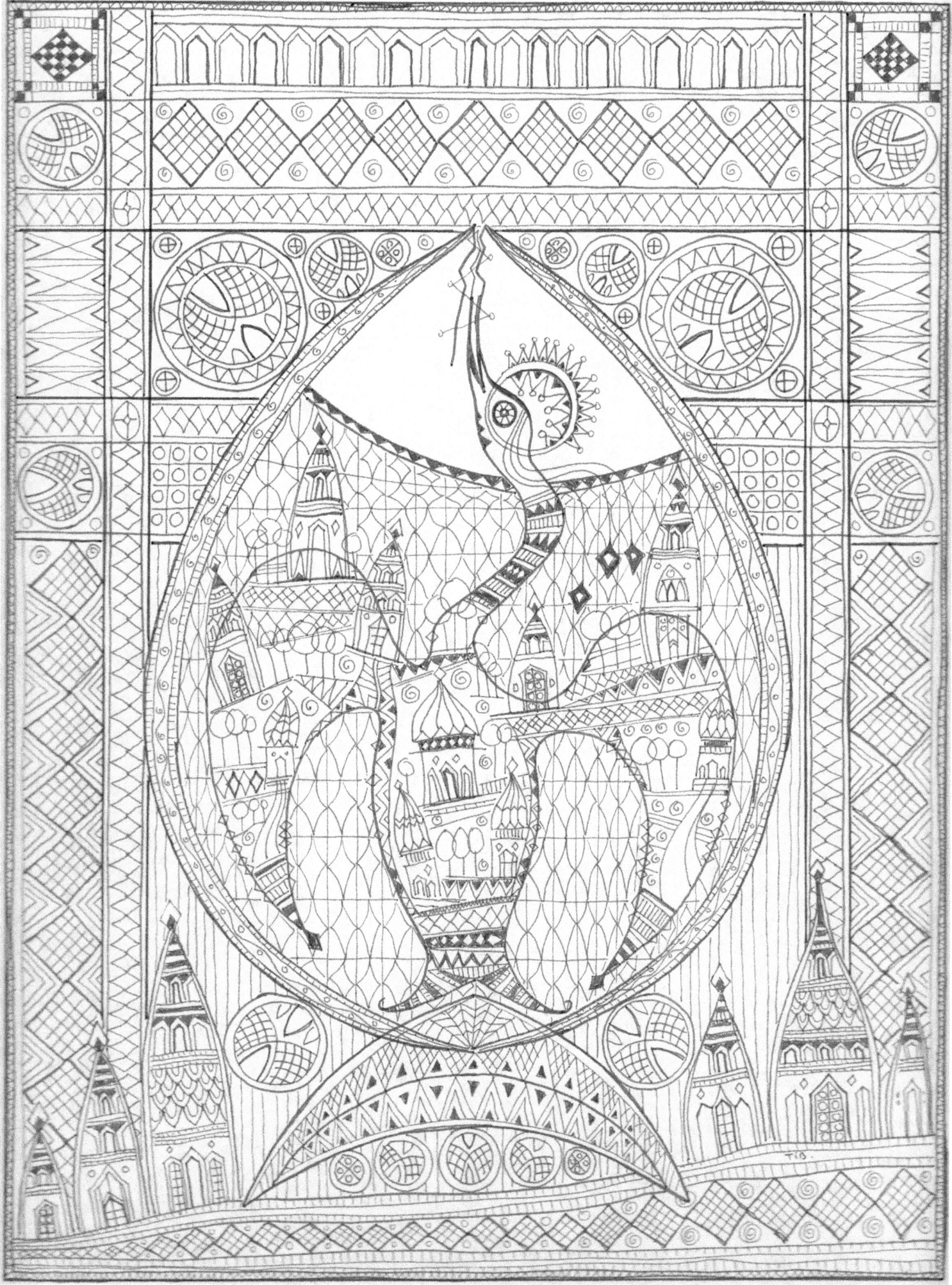

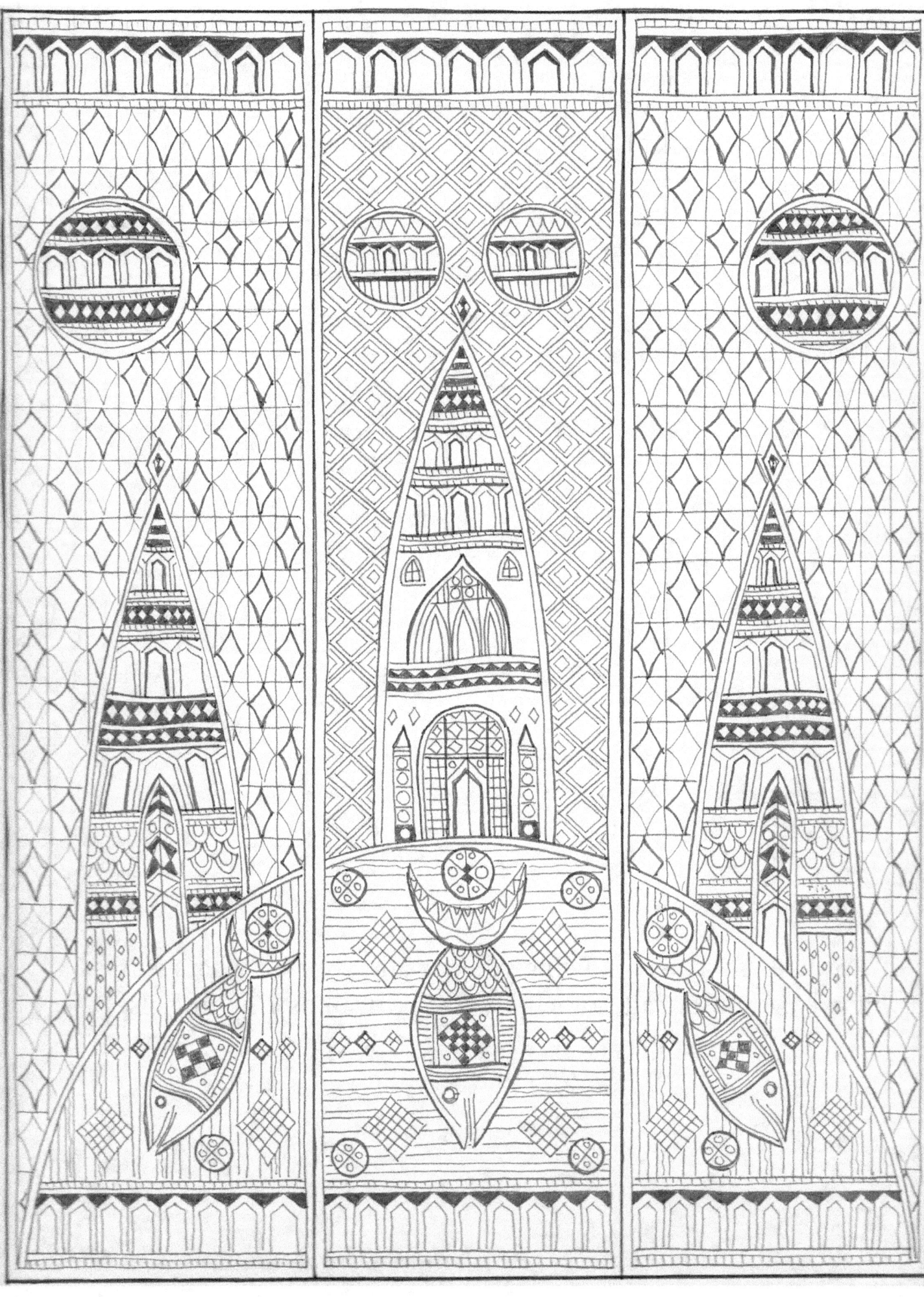

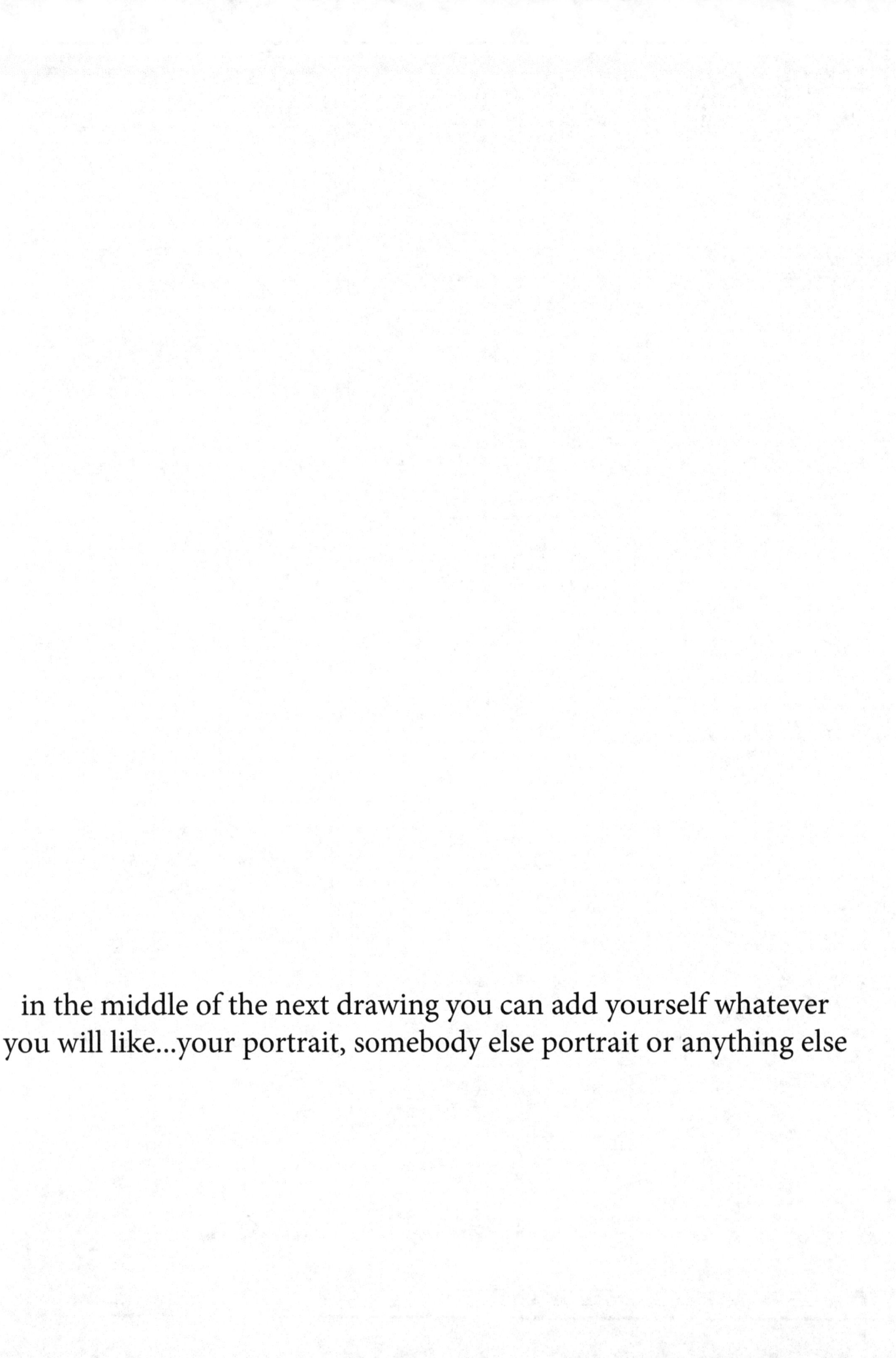

in the middle of the next drawing you can add yourself whatever
you will like...your portrait, somebody else portrait or anything else

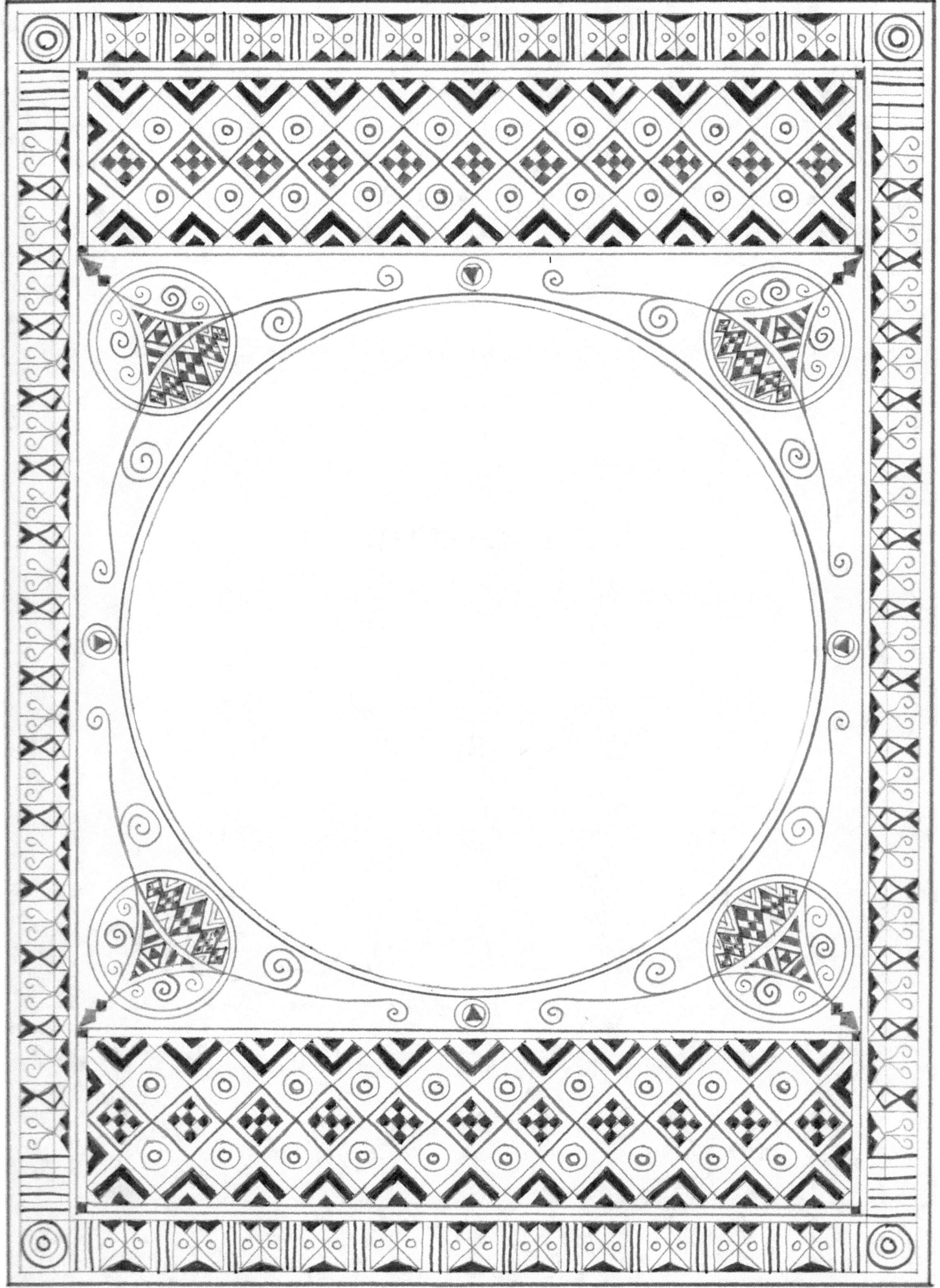

THE END OF THIS
BOOK

by

JULIAN TROCARU

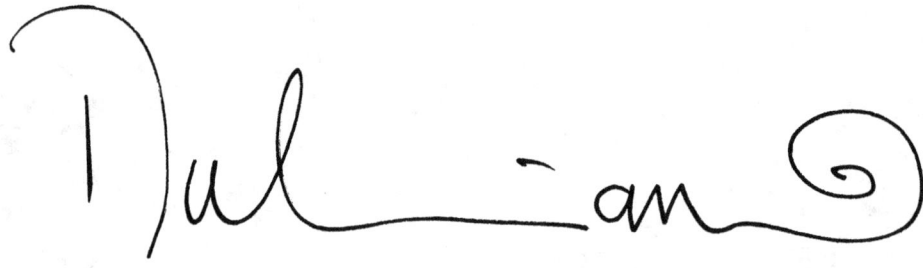

www.ingramcontent.com/pod-product-compliance
Lightning Source LLC
Chambersburg PA
CBHW080822180526
45168CB00006B/2545